萌えるれ〜！
そいつは幽霊だ!!

PARANORMAL SCIENCE NVL
Occultic;Nine
オカルティック・ナイン

THERE IS NO SUCH THING AS THE "OCCULT." IT CAN ALL BE DISPROVED BY SCIENCE.
ONLY THOSE WHO HAVE ACCEPTED EVERYTHING
HAVE THE RIGHT TO KNOW THE TRUTH.

01

CHIYOMARU SHIKURA
art by **pako**

That was my first meeting with the strange girl named "Ryotasu"...

"I-shi-shu! Hands to the sky, pardner!"

Then suddenly something was pointing at the side of my head. Out of the corner of my eye I could just barely make out a silver... was that a handgun?

Yuta Gamon
Website Admin, Student

Ryoka Narusawa
Gun Girl, Huge Boobs,
Student

Sarai Hashigam
Scientist, Student

Miyuu
Aikawa
Fortune Teller,
Celebrity Student

Aria
Kurenaino
Black Magic Agent

Kiryu
Kusakabe
Out of Body Experiencer,
Bill Collector

Toko Sumikaze
Spiritualist,
Magazine Writer

Ririka Nishizono
Doujin Manga Author

Shun Moritsuka
Mentalist, Detective

PARANORMAL SCIENCE NVL

Occultic;Nine

オカルティック・ナイン

THERE IS NO SUCH THING AS THE "OCCULT." IT CAN ALL BE DISPROVED BY SCIENCE.
ONLY THOSE WHO HAVE ACCEPTED EVERYTHING
HAVE THE RIGHT TO KNOW THE TRUTH.

01

Presented by
CHIYOMARU SHIKURA

Illustrated by
pako

Seven Seas

novel club

OCCULTIC;NINE, VOLUME 1

© 2013 SHIKURA CHIYOMARU
© 2013 pako

First published in Japan in 2014 by
OVERLAP Inc., Ltd., Tokyo.
English translation rights arranged with
OVERLAP Inc., Ltd., Tokyo.

Seven Seas books may be purchased in bulk for promotional,
educational, or business use. Please contact your local
bookseller or the Macmillan Corporate and Premium Sales
Department at 1-800-221-7945, extension 5442, or by
e-mail at MacmillanSpecialMarkets@macmillan.com.

Follow Seven Seas Entertainment online at gomanga.com.
Experience J-Novel Club books online at j-novel.club.

Translation: Adam Lensenmayer
J-Novel Editor: Alicia Ashby
Book Layout: Karis Page
Cover Design: Nicky Lim
Copy Editor: Tom Speelman
Light Novel Editor: Jenn Grunigen
Production Assistant: CK Russell
Production Manager: Lissa Pattillo
Editor-in-Chief: Adam Arnold
Publisher: Jason DeAngelis

ISBN: 978-1-626926-59-2
Printed in Canada
First Printing: July 2017
10 9 8 7 6 5 4 3 2 1

CONTENTS

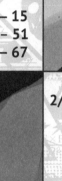

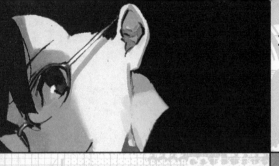

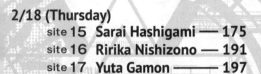

超常科学NVL
Occultic;Nine

THERE ARE NO SUCH THING AS "OCCULT". IT CAN BE DISPROVED ALL BY SCIENCE.
ONLY THE ONES WHO HAVE ACCEPTED EVERYTHING
CAN GET THE RIGHT TO KNOW THE TRUTH!

Leafless trees shook and shuddered, battered by the wind coming down from above.

Several helicopters circled in the sky, their rotors loudly beating against the air.

The motors of heavy equipment groaned.

Dozens of men yelled to each other as they dredged the lake.

In the distance, there were ambulance sirens.

It all overlapped into a giant, obnoxious wall of sound.

All the noise was coming from Inokashira Park.

No, the whole town of Kichijoji had been noisy and on edge today. There was a strange sense of excitement and oppression that you could see on the faces of the people on the streets.

Inokashira Park was normally a place for the locals to relax, but now it was blocked off by police tape and torn apart by construction equipment.

A power shovel was parked as close as it could possibly get to the lake, its arm sticking into the water.

There were dozens of men around it, all wearing work clothes.

The lake itself was filled with men on rubber boats dredging the water.

Even people who had lived here for years had never seen anything like this.

Every year at about this time, the city of Musashino would dredge up all the trash from Inokashira Lake, but this year it was different.

The backhoe slowly raised its scoop from the water's depths.

It pulled up what looked like lumpy bags of garbage and added them to the pile forming around the lake.

Inokashira Lake was ringed with a mountain of garbage.

There was far more garbage than usual this year.

It was garbage thrown out by a small number of arrogant, ill-mannered men.

Garbage created by the unethical and selfish.

Sad garbage.

The garbage of society.

Garbage, garbage, garbage, garbage, garbage, garbage, garbage...

But it wasn't just garbage. It was dead bodies.

"Can you see something that looks like a face? Then it's a ghost picture."
From Modern Entertainment

A photo uploaded by a certain Twitter user had the whole internet in an uproar.

It was a photo taken somewhere in the city, and get this: They say it's a ghost photo.

The photographer himself noticed a few days after he'd taken the photo that, indeed, it was possible to see a male face contorted in pain in the grass behind him.

■NEET God
A MALE FACE lololol CONTORTED IN PAIN lolol

You see something that looks like a face and you figure it's gotta be a ghost. Right. Got it. You know, how come ghosts always just show their faces? Why do they never show up stark naked? How come it's never some hot ghost-slut with huge tits, spread legs, an o-face and a double peace sign? Anybody got any ghost photos like that? Lol

If you do, I'm ready to start believing! Lolol
Okay, Basariters, rip it apart.
Oh, or if there's any self-proclaimed spiritualists out there, your expert opinion is always welcome lol

1: True Tales of Anonymous

I've seen this photo. It's famous. Oh and FIRST.

2: True Tales of Anonymous

Yeah, that sure looks like a face, I guess. And 2chan says the guy who took the picture still feels all heavy and he's getting chills and stuff. Can't these people ever come up with anything new? Somebody tell him how to do an exorcism! I'm half-srs.

3: True Tales of Anonymous

The hell is this? Scary. This is way more than just a coincidence.

4: True Tales of Anonymous

Admin you're shit and this is old news. People were talking about this two months ago, dumbass.

6: True Tales of Anonymous

That's true. There are some where you can see faces though.

8: True Tales of Anonymous

What are the odds it's photoshopped?

10: True Tales of Anonymous

Mulder, you're tired.

13: True Tales of Anonymous

>10

I lol'd.

20: True Tales of Anonymous

I know this place. It's where a killer murdered someone and chopped their body into tiny little pieces. I don't want to say where exactly so I'll block out some of the letters: Inoka**ira Park.

23: True Tales of Anonymous

>20
Inoka**ira Park? Lol who the hell do you think you're fooling.

28: True Tales of Anonymous

>23
You mean you cracked my brilliant code?!
30: True Tales of Anonymous
Oh shit. That's right next door.

35: True Tales of Anonymous

So what, the photo's real then? If it's real that's scary as fuck. Tell me, NEET God!

37: True Tales of Anonymous

This is "Kirikiri Basara," right?

38: True Tales of Anonymous

Of course it's not real, lol. Any moron with a computer can make a ghost photo these days. How dumb do you have to be to get scared of this?

40: True Tales of Anonymous

Right, right. There's no such thing as ghosts. Someone make the scary go away!

My fingers came down hard on the laptop's keyboard.

I couldn't get my thoughts out fast enough. It was aggravating that I couldn't type faster. There were so many thoughts I wanted to get out there. Why did it have to take so much work? Life was hard.

"You know what an affiliate blog is, right? There's no better profession out there for my NEET friends. Basically, the more popular your blog, the more hits you get. And the more people who click on your affiliate links, the more money you earn."

Oops, I was speaking out loud as I typed. Well, nothing wrong with that.

"It's the American dream, I guess you could say. Oh, you can google the forms you need to sign up for an affiliate program. It's easy enough—so I'll skip the explanation here. Sorry. But it's simple enough that your average salaryman or housewife can do it as a second job."

I was on Twitter. There were a ton of eggs there who loved to give me a hard time. And the vast majority were idiots who would always take things out of context.

"My name is the NEET God and I run a site called Paranormal Science Kirikiri Basara, where I find interesting articles on news sites and individual blogs, then summarize them in my own unique, cool, and classy way."

Right now I was politely explaining to these idiots how the blog I ran worked.

"But there's really a trick to how you pick your articles. And unfortunately, 2ch doesn't let you reproduce stuff from their site, so you can't take anything from there."

From the perspective of me and the other aggregate site owners, the founder of 2chan, Hiroyuki, had a pretty annoying policy. I wanted to ride the big wave, too!

I found myself getting a little irritated, so I took a big drink of water to calm down. The ice in the glass had almost melted and a single drop fell onto my pants and left a mark. The heater was running, so even in the winter, cold water felt good.

"Basically, I'm a normal 2nd-year NEET student in high school who wants to up his affiliate income and get rich, like others have done before me. But I'm not making enough money for you to be jealous over. I'm making so little that I want to kill myself. Maybe I was an idiot for picking a site like this just because occult stuff has been popular lately. There are so many other copycat sites like mine that my hit counter is basically frozen."

And then, even my followers who weren't eggs started to chime in. Most of their comments were along the lines of, "People who try to make pocket change off affiliate links should be taken out into the street and shot," and, "Don't worry, I'm never clicking on anything on your site." I was getting really tired of seeing that.

What was so wrong about trying to make money off affiliate links? It wasn't like it was illegal or anything. These guys were just jealous because they couldn't make a good site!

But if I said that, it'd only add fuel to the flame war, so I didn't.

People on the internet got mad whenever you were right and they weren't. If starting a flame war was a good way to up my affiliate income, I wouldn't mind. But honestly, it wasn't.

"Oh, but my top priority is always providing my Basariters with top-quality content! I look forward to seeing you guys rip some stuff apart today!"

That was how I decided to end it.

Of course, what I, Yuta Gamon, was actually trying to say was, "Visit my site more and buy more stuff from my affiliate links." Man, I couldn't wait until I made enough off affiliate links to survive. These days, only losers had real jobs.

That was how I planned to end it anyway, but then the eggs refused to shut up.

"Creepy otaku virgins like you who refuse to get jobs don't even have the right to breathe, let alone walk around outside."

"I'll cop to being an otaku and a virgin, but I'm not creepy. If I try to blend in, my looks are above average. At least, that's what I think."

I had no intentions of saying I was a good-looking guy, but I was more attractive than your average NEET. At least, that's what I wanted to believe.

I heard a loud, instantly recognizable laugh from behind me. A solidly built, well-muscled man stood behind the counter, chortling.

"You know, Gamota, you might have above-average looks, but they go to waste when you bury your face in a duffel coat and mumble to yourself, you know?"

"Grrr…" I couldn't let myself talk back to him.

He was the owner of the café. If I ticked him off, I might lose my base of operations.

The name of this place was Café ☆ Blue Moon. To get here, you'd go out the north side of Kichijoji Station, take the street behind the Yodobashi store, then walk past a bunch of love hotels. It was only a five-minute walk from the station, but it still had the feeling of a secret hideout. At night it was a bar, but during the day it was a café.

The place had an exotic, Oriental atmosphere, due to all the items around the café that the owner had personally purchased on his travels around the world. Of course, an "exotic, Oriental atmosphere" sounded good in theory, but none of the tables and chairs matched at all, and it was a little bewildering to look at. Rococo-style chairs were lined up next to ones made from wicker and there was a little Japanese-style room filled with cushions shaped like chocolate pies.

What was he *going* for with all this?

But there were two reasons I liked this place. First, other students almost never came here. And second, it had a grown-up atmosphere.

Also, you could sit here for hours without ordering anything but water, and he wouldn't get mad or kick you out. That was nice, too.

I leaned back in the wicker sofa, then turned toward the owner and raised my empty glass.

"Master Izumin, may I have some more water?"

"Oh, jeez, you're working me to the bone, honey."

His real name was Kohei Izumi, and he was 43 years old. His nickname was Izumin. That's what he'd told me to call him. His high-pitched, effeminate manner of speaking, his soft bearing, and the fact that he always wore makeup might lead you to make certain assumptions, but according to him none of those were true.

He mumbled some complaints to himself as he poured me a new glass of water. I took it and turned back to my laptop.

"Wait, Gamota, shouldn't you be at school?"

"There's no school today."

"Oh, is it? Oh dear. Oh my stars! I've lost track of what day it is!"

My school, Seimei High, was about twenty minutes away on foot. For what it was worth, that was also about the same distance to my house. In other words, Kichijoji was my hometown. And on my days off, instead of staying at home, I always went outside to avoid living the traditional NEET lifestyle.

I was more of an active NEET.

"You know, Gamota, I saw that Kirikiri Barber site or whatever it's called. I have to say, if you keep making fun of ghosts, you're going to regret it. The occult is real. And don't come running to little old Izumin when you need somebody to save you! 'Cause I won't!"

"I laugh at your curses! I lol at them! There are no such things as ghosts."

I didn't believe in the occult at all. That was Kirikiri Basara's official stance. Of course, in a horror movie, whoever said that was always the first to die.

"You know, Master Izumin, Kirikiri Basara isn't just your typical aggregator site. It's a site where we take all the world's occult phenomena and go, '*Ha ha!* I'll prove you wrong!'"

The name had come from the words "kiri" or "cut," and "basara," which meant "to not hold back." It's just a silly name I made up one day when I'd gotten mad at something but I don't regret it. The Basariters who commented on my site were even more brutal about this stuff than I was, after all. I actually think I was pretty lucky to come up with it.

Of course, as an individual, I wasn't sure how I thought about that. It put me in a bad position as site admin, after all. But whenever one of the Basariters commented, it always meant a lot of hits. Since my goal was to make a living off my affiliate links, I couldn't chase them out.

The door opened and a girl I instantly recognized came spinning in like a ballet dancer.

"Gamotan! ♪ Gamotan goes ♪♪ Ribbit-ribbit-ribbit like a frog! ♪"

"I do not."

Her steps were beautiful and fluid, even if her song was out of tune. She hopped a few times, spun around, and then swayed. There was no logic to her movement. She was in thrall to the impulses that came from deep within her.

And damned if her boobs weren't bouncing! Her gigantic, watermelon-sized boobs!

"Gamotan! ♪"

YES! I wanted to make a video and watch it every night before bed. I didn't even bother saying anything about her weird dance, opting instead to pump my fist in joy where no one could see it.

But damn, if I watched any more, I was going to get a nosebleed.

"Stop! Okay, okay! Stop dancing!" I turned toward the dancing boob-angel, clapping my hands and shouting, like a choreographer on one of those reality TV shows.

"Poyaya?"

"Don't say 'poyaya,' Ryotasu." Ryotasu was what I called her. More precisely, Ryotasu was what she called herself, and I simply took it from her.

Of course, it was just a nickname. Her real name was Ryoka Narusawa. She was a year younger than me, and went to Seimei High, just like I did.

She was one of my few friends in the real world, and also helped as an employee of Kirikiri Basara.

I considered myself extremely lucky to be friends with a younger girl like her. At school, I was a weirdo who wasn't part of anybody's social group, and online I was so disliked that I got mocked by eggs on Twitter. But that didn't matter, did it?

Just the fact that Ryotasu was here made me far superior to my classmates who spent all their time in school clubs, or the unemployed thirty-somethings who spent all their time on the internet all day. I was practically normal.

In other words, Ryotasu's role within the party was to give me a major status buff. She was cute, she had huge tits, and—

"You know, your real job isn't dancing. It's working for Kirikiri Basara. Help me deal with these stupid eggs..."

"Cock-a-doodle-doo? If you want an egg, go to a hen! ♪ If you want a meal, go to a rooster! ♪ Cock-a-doodle-doo! ♪"

...And she was also a little...*odd*.

When she finished her song, she spun around toward Master Izumin and took a bow. The wonderful show had come to an end.

Ryotasu did whatever Ryotasu wanted. There were times when she'd just burst into song for no reason other than that she felt like it. What she was doing a moment ago, or what she might be doing a moment later, didn't matter in the slightest.

Ryotasu spun around once more to face me and then leaned her face in close. It was so close, I almost flinched back.

"You know, the whole point of Kirikiri Basara is to make you rich—right, Gamotan? But I don't get any money, right?"

She stared straight into my eyes. She was staring too deeply! I was going to fall in love!

"O-okay, when I get the money from the affiliate links, I'll buy you some suta-don. I recommend the soy-garlic flavor. Oh, or would you prefer salt and garlic?"

That was my way of paying her. A bowl of suta-don was a cheap price to pay.

"Hmm...I'd rather have some frozen yogurt from Woodberrys."

"W-Woodberrys?"

"It's a frozen yogurt shop near the station!"

"H-huh..."

I'd lived in Kichijoji for years, but I'd never gone to any fancy places like that. I deliberately avoided them, in fact.

"All right, that works."

"Yay! I'll do my best, then!"

Ryotasu leapt up to express her joy.

I couldn't stop my eyes from following the bouncing breasts in front of me.

Up then down.

And then up again.

An infinite loop.

"Amazing."

"Hmm? What is?"

"Never change!"

"Aye-aye, sir! ☆"

Ryotasu raised her right hand, smiled, and saluted.

You know, Ryotasu always wore clothes that emphasized her chest. I loved it. Those were total boob-bags. I thought those things only existed in H-games. Not that I'd ever played one.

And then there was another interruption from the counter.

"Gamota, you're staring."

"Hey! You're a much bigger pervert than I am, Master Izumin!"

"Yup, that's right!" Ryotasu agreed. I was happy she understood.

"What do you mean, 'That's right'? Why? Why? WHY? Ryotasu, how could you agree with him?"

"Poyaya?" Ryotasu crossed her arms below her chest and tilted her head, making a pose like she was thinking. "Poyaya" was probably another one of her meaningless phrases. She had different phrases that she used depending on her situation and mood.

I would've preferred she speak in Japanese but it was still cute. Everything about Ryotasu was cute. And since she was cute, it was okay.

Ryotasu sat down next to me, still maintaining her thinking pose. She was looking up at the ceiling—or so I thought, until I felt a toy ray gun poking me in the ribs. The Poyaya Gun, she always called it.

"Hey, hey, Samurai Gamonosuke!"

Who the hell was Samurai Gamonosuke? No one had ever called me that in my life.

And anyway, her face was way too close. She was asking for a kiss! She had to be! Ryotasu was in love with me! But her face was still way too close!

"Um... Ryotasu?"

"Po-ya?"

"You're too close."

"Poyaya?"

"Distance-wise."

"Poyah."

I didn't know what she was saying, but she seemed to understand me and backed away a little. The ray gun was still poking into my ribs, though.

"Hey, hey, when do I get my frozen yogurt?"

"Well, once I get my affiliate money in, I guess."

I decided to look and see when that would be.

"Today's view count is...*NGGAAH!*" Some famous affiliate blogs got hundreds of thousands of hits a day. Compared to that, my numbers made me want to jump off a bridge.

"Monthly view count is...*MGHAH!*" That number was just as bad.

Unless I did something about these numbers, I could probably make a heck of a lot more money working at that frozen yogurt place.

"I guess the real money's in porn... But wait. God controls all things. Someday, occult sites shall surpass erotic sites!"

"God is Ero-him Essaim, after all!" Ryotasu put her hands together in prayer and wiggled and contorted her body.

As I watched her shake her body out of the corner of my eye, I slammed my finger down on the F5 key. "Hitting the button sixteen times isn't really going to change my view numbers, though!"

The numbers weren't exactly zero, but some months, the deposit fees ate up all my money. I had a long way to go to achieve my goal of being an independent NEET.

"Our views aren't going up very fast. We've got a long way to go before all-you-can-eat frozen yogurt, Ryotasu."

"I see..." Ryotasu looked depressed. "My yogurt..."

I felt bad, but there wasn't anything I could do about it, so I decided to ignore her.

I checked the blog.

There were more comments now.

"Wait, is it him again?"

"That's right! His name is... S! A! R! A! I! SARAI!"

"Yes..."

Sarai was a regular commenter at Kirikiri Basara, and the smartest one we had.

To be honest, most of the debunking work on the site was done by him. He was someone I could count on.

In fact, whenever Sarai showed up and commented, the view count would go up a little as people came to read it. So while I felt grateful as the owner of the site, I did feel a little jealous that I wasn't the star of my own show.

Male pride was a complicated thing.

"Oh, whoops. I'm getting emotional."

I read through Sarai's comment with the usual mixture of dread and anticipation. The page was filled with one of his usual long comments.

"This photo is a typical example of a simulacrum. I can say, without the slightest doubt, that this is not a spirit photograph, and what's more, most so-called spirit photographs can be entirely explained via the simulacrum phenomenon, which is also known as the pareidolia effect."

"tl; dr."

"Wow, Sarai is always so amazing, huh?"

Hmm?! Ryotasu's eyes were wide with amazement as she read Sarai's debunking.

I know you have to look over to read the screen, but Ryotasu, your face is really close! I thought. *And your boobs! They're touching me! They're touching me and I can't focus on what Sarai's saying!*

If you were to make a pie chart of all the thoughts in my head at that moment, it would have been 3% happiness that my views had gone up, and 6% annoyance that Sarai was stealing my thunder, with the remaining 91% of me going, "Ryotasu! You're too close to me again!"

I was so excited, I almost forgot about the site!

"Oh! Gamotan's got a naughty look on his face!" Ryotasu suddenly said.

"Huh?! What do you mean, 'a naughty look'?! I do not!"

"Naughty Gamotans get I-shi-shu!" Ryotasu pointed the ray gun in her hand at me and pulled the trigger.

I felt a sharp pain and numbness run through my whole body.

"Ow! Ow, ow, ow!" When you were hit with the PYG—at least, that's what I called her Poyaya Gun—you felt a stinging sensation like an electrostim treatment.

It didn't shoot rays but I was sure it shot some kind of electromagnetic pulse.

"Wait! Stop! PYG! No!"

"I-SHI-SHU!"

I had no idea what that meant, but Ryotasu sure was excited.

She still kept shooting even after I fell out of my chair and started writhing on the ground. Maybe she was actually a huge sadist?

"Ow! Ow! Ow! That hurts! Fine, I'll stop imagining naughty things!"

Satisfied, Ryotasu finally put away her gun.

"Gahh... Hahh... Hahh... Whew..."

Wh-what jackass gave a girl like Ryotasu a (semi-)deadly weapon?

It was her fault for always getting right up in my face, anyway. What gave her the right to shoot me just because I looked like I enjoyed it? Not that I wanted her to stop.

"Aw, it's good to see you two kids flirting like that." Master Izumin had a creepy grin on his face as he teased me.

But it didn't bother me. I bet any other guy would kill to get a chance to play with Ryotasu like this. I sat back in my chair, feeling like a winner.

Sarai's comment was still displayed on the screen. I glanced through the rest of it.

"The simulacrum phenomenon is one of the brain and eye's most basic functions. When the eye sees dots or lines arranged in a triangular shape, the brain interprets them as a face. This is an animal instinct that every person is born with. Since there are several such dots and lines in the photograph, it's even easier for the brain to interpret them as faces. However, if you look at each portion individually, you'll see that they're all tricks of the light or part of the background."

"I'm convinced. But I hate to admit it. But I'm convinced," someone else replied.

I looked away from the monitor and rubbed my eyes again. Sarai's comments were so complicated that I always felt tired reading them.

"You can tell from the way he writes that he thinks he's smarter than everyone, you know? I bet he thinks that everybody in the world but him is stupid. If he's this smart, and he's got a girlfriend and she's really hot, I'll never forgive him. Ever."

Ryotasu suddenly looked off into the distance when she heard my "profiling."

"I feel bad for poor Sarai."

"Y-you feel bad for him?!"

What did that mean?

My heart almost stopped for a second there.

"Ryotasu, you know Sarai?"

"Sure do! I always read his comments on Kirikiri Basara. Not all the way through, though. Ehehe..."

"No, I mean, do you know him in real life?"

"I don't know him in real life! ♪"

"Oh, okay..."

So it was just her imagination, then?

Still, "poor Sarai," huh? I had no idea where she was getting that from his comments.

I didn't see any comments from Sarai yet on the newer articles. There was always a big lag between when I'd post a new article and when he'd comment on it. He was probably spending a lot of time doing research, like your typical nerd.

I'd put up three new articles on Kirikiri Basara today: "Man Livestreams One-Man Hide and Seek, Never Comes Back," "The Curse of Kokkuri-san Is Seriously Terrifying," and "Is It True That a Girl Once Lived with a Mummy?" I'd uploaded all of them since I'd come to the café this morning. Since all three of them had supposedly occurred in Kichijoji, I'd taken to calling them the Kichijoji Trilogy.

They'd been up for hours but Sarai would probably wait until tomorrow to comment. Aside from Sarai, how many other people had commented by now? I decided to take a look.

"Man Livestreams One-Man Hide and Seek, Never Comes Back!"
From J-Cast News

There's a certain video on Niconico that's attracting a lot of attention.

It's a livestream of a man performing a ritual called "One-Man Hide and Seek," as described in urban legends.

Get this: there's a rumor that after the broadcast, the streamer vanished!

The video is approximately three hours in length and consists of nothing but footage of a doll sitting in the streamer's room. Nothing special seems to happen. But after the upload, the streamer, who had regularly been tweeting 100+ times a day, stopped tweeting altogether. And a woman believed to be the man's sister wrote on her own blog that her brother had suddenly vanished.

Upon noticing this, one of the streamer's followers contacted the Musashino area police, who confirmed that a missing person report had been filed for him.

■ NEET God

The whole thing sounds like a setup to me, lol.

And what's more, J-Cast just ripped this whole thing off of 2ch.

And what's with all these livestreams of One-Man Hide and Seek, anyway?

There's like a billion of the things.

What's that? "Explain One-Man Hide and Seek"?

Lmgtfy, jackass.

Okay, Basariters, rip it apart.

1: Anonymous FOUND YOU

FIRST POST, BITCHES!

2: Anonymous FOUND YOU

Snake, what's wrong? Snake? SNAAKKKKEEEE!

4: Anonymous FOUND YOU

We don't even know for sure that the guy on the missing person report is the same guy as the streamer.

Where do people get this shit? Lol

7: Anonymous FOUND YOU

>4

2ch figured out that guy lived in Kichijoji, which is in Musashino. After that they saw a missing person report in the newspaper for a guy in Musashino, and then it hit the news sites.

18: Anonymous FOUND YOU

You guys don't honestly think this is real, right? Dude's probably just trying to run from some bad debts or something.

32: Anonymous FOUND YOU

NEET God, stop putting up these crappy articles all the time.

37: Anonymous FOUND YOU

>18

But from the photos I saw, he'd put some real effort into setting it up. It's obvious he was pretty serious about doing the livestream.

41: Anonymous FOUND YOU

Affiliate – Affiliate – Affiliate – Affiliate – Affiliate – Affiliate – Affiliate – Affiliate – Affiliate – Affiliate – Affiliate – Affiliate – Affiliate – Affiliate – Affiliate – Affiliate – Affiliate – Affiliate

43: Anonymous FOUND YOU

Man this stuff was old news ages ago. Who gives a crap about Solo Hide-and-Seek these days NEET God, get with the times, damn it.

47: Anonymous FOUND YOU

It's okay to trip.
It's okay to fall.
It's okay to play hide-and-seek.

That's what it means to be human.
By Mitsuwo

53: Anonymous FOUND YOU

If the guy who went missing in Musashino really is the guy from the Solo Hide-and-Seek video, wouldn't this be bigger news?

59: Anonymous FOUND YOU

No way is the news gonna talk about this stuff. Since when does the mainstream media cover anything occult?

72: Anonymous FOUND YOU

I laughed when I found out that there are as many variants for the rules of One-Man Hide and Seek as there are for rules of poker.

"The Curse of Kokkuri-san Is Seriously Terrifying!"
From Twitter

@shimizuBBA

I heard from someone in my club that four girls from the third-year class were playing Kokkuri-san, and one of them took her finger off the board. She ended up going crazy and they had to take her to the hospital. There was an ambulance at school sometime during the fall. So that's what that was? Scary!

▪ NEET God

The source is Twitter, home of the stupidest people on the internet. Okay, Basariters, rip it apart.

9: Anonymous is Seriously Scary

Kokkuri-san is like a Japanese ouija board. It scares the hell out of me.

12: Anonymous is Seriously Scary

Obvious BS, lol. But I like this stuff about a Kichijoji high school girl, so feel free to keep going.

13: Anonymous is Seriously Scary

Kokkuri-san = Ko (Fox), Ku (Dog) Ri (Raccoon).

20: Anonymous is Seriously Scary

My grandma caught me playing Kokkuri-san once and started screaming at me. She told me to never, ever play it. She's dead now, though.

21: Anonymous is Seriously Scary

Why are all these articles from Kichijoji, lol. Is that place cursed or something? This place is turning into a local newspaper.

24: Anonymous is Seriously Scary

She's currently locked in a psych ward and they're not letting her receive visitors.
Source: A friend who goes to the same school.

34: Anonymous is Seriously Scary.

>24
You're obviously NEET God using an alt. You're fooling nobody. You don't need to make crap up to try and make this more exciting, lol

39: Anonymous is Seriously Scary

Don't you use a 5-yen piece to play Kokkuri-san? In the age of digital currency I bet the ghosts are bored off their asses (@_@)

42: Anonymous is Seriously Scary

Just use your Suica card that you use for the trains.

46: Anonymous is Seriously Scary

>42
I bet it makes that "ding" noise when it stops over a certain letter.

48: Anonymous is Seriously Scary

Stop it, you'll open the automatic turnstile to the spirit world! Lol

51: Anonymous is Seriously Scary

More like COCK-kuri-san iykwimaityd

53: Anonymous is Seriously Scary

I looked up how the hell stuff like Kokkuri-san and ouija boards actually work and it's a kind of group hypnosis. Maybe it really is that scary. Post-hypnotic suggestions and mind control are real, after all.

57: Anonymous is Seriously Scary

I don't believe in hypnosis and mind control, anyway. I'm sure it wouldn't work on me lol

"Is It True That a Girl Once Lived with a Mummy?"
From the Tokyo Urban Legends Blog

Did you know that there's a huge mansion that's been unoccupied for years in a corner of a Kichijoji residential district?

Several years ago, a mummified corpse was found there. The TV shows were all over it.

It seems the body belonged to a resident of the mansion who died from an illness.

But there's actually a terrifying rumor surrounding the incident.

There was another person who was living with the mummy in the mansion: a girl who was only 14 or 15 years old!

■ **NEET God**
A loli who lives with a mummy lol.
It sounds like an H-game.
When's the movie version coming?
Okay, Basariters, rip it apart.

1: Anonymous lives 24/7 in his mom's basement
FROST PRIST

3: Anonymous lives 24/7 in his mom's basement
http://www.love*lovedeaiknews.com/archive13/

5: Anonymous lives 24/7 in his mom's basement
So the mummy was banging the girl, right?

6: Anonymous lives 24/7 in his mom's basement
For the first time in my life, I want to be a mummy.

7: Anonymous lives 24/7 in his mom's basement
Let's go to the sea, Brother. You love the sea, right?

10: Anonymous lives 24/7 in his mom's basement
>7
That's right. You put the dried mummy in the sea and it puffs up, and goes back to being a person. Wait, that's dried seaweed!

12: Anonymous lives 24/7 in his mom's basement
Guys you're missing the most important part. They found a mummy

in some family's house! And this girl was hiding it from the cops! And the body had gone missing from a hospital after the guy had died there! That's a crime!

16: Anonymous lives 24/7 in his mom's basement

You've got me there. I bet the hospital was trying to keep it...under wraps!

21: Anonymous lives 24/7 in his mom's basement

"Mummy" is a bad way to put it. "Mummified body" is better.

24: Anonymous lives 24/7 in his mom's basement

I bet he was just lonely, and wanted his MUMMY. haha. Get it?

27: Anonymous lives 24/7 in his mom's basement

If you've got a thing for bandaged chicks, you'll love mummies.

31: Anonymous lives 24/7 in his mom's basement

I thought mummies only had bandages in anime.

35: Anonymous lives 24/7 in his mom's basement

I'm pretty sure that some Egyptian mummies have bandages and some don't. (^^)

42: Anonymous lives 24/7 in his mom's basement

So who took the body from the hospital to the house, and why? Is there a source somewhere?

"Gah... I hate to say it, but without that nerd Sarai, the rest of them are all morons."

I softly closed the lid of my laptop and let out a long, long sigh.

"I'm feeling extremely tired all of a sudden. Let's get some food. I've been working all day and I'm starving."

"Working? You?"

"That's right. I'm the site admin."

Ryotasu tilted her head in confusion as she checked the time on the cuckoo clock on the wall. The little hand was past the four.

"You didn't eat lunch?"

"I didn't eat lunch and I didn't eat breakfast either."

Mom had been out working and wasn't there when I woke up again. My mom's job didn't really give her days off.

"Oh, but you don't really eat a lot, do you, Gamota? Are you just one of those boys who doesn't eat?"

I could hear Master Izumin's sarcastic voice from behind the counter. I activated my "ignore" skill to completely shut out the sound of his voice.

"Gamotan, Gamotan! If you only eat one meal a day, you'll get fat—like a sumo wrestler. Plumpy and dumpy! ☆"

"NEETs are either super-thin, or super-fat. I'm the former, so I'll be fine."

"I see! ☆"

Ryotasu brought her face up so close that I thought she might be trying to head-butt me. Her eyes were shining as she looked in mine.

"Y-you're too close." What was so interesting about what I just said, anyway? I didn't understand why Ryotasu found that impressive. It was a mystery.

I waited but Ryotasu refused to move her face away. So I looked down, awkwardly.

I saw my bag near my feet. Strictly speaking, it wasn't a bag. It was a laptop case with a built-in shoulder strap. I'd made it myself.

My Zonko strap, from MMM (*Master Must Murder*), shook as I lifted it up and put it on my lap.

Yup. Pretty cute.

Inside the case was my BCL (Broadcast Listener) radio, which I always kept with me. This was a powerful radio that let me listen to international shortwave broadcasts. It was a model called a Skysensor. I didn't come up with that. I would've come up with a less geeky name. That was just the name of the product.

Dad had given it to me when he was still alive. It was quite an antique since it had been manufactured in 1975. But I thought it had a sleek, modern design that didn't really look old at all.

You didn't have to be a radio hobbyist to love this design. Any kid would love it. In fact, it had been popular with both kids and adults. I felt like I knew why.

Its body was the size of a large bento box, and heavy. Its main tuning dial and bandspread dials were big and sturdy, like the dials on a safe at the bank. The frequency panel had the numbers carved into it. There were switches to move between AM and FM, and to turn the device on and off.

It was fun just to play with the dials and switches, even if you weren't actually doing anything.

Ryotasu was watching me as I moved my hands. She was so close, I could almost feel her breath.

I turned on the power switch. White noise came out of the speaker.

--PWWEEEWWW-----BZZT

Just listening to the sound of the white noise made me feel nostalgic, and kind of special.

I spun the dial at random.

Don't look at the saved settings. Don't rely on your ears, either. Just feel it with your hands.

That's what Dad taught me, I think. The sound coming out of the speakers was constantly changing, and you could actually *feel* it in the tips of your fingers as you touched the dial. That was one of the unique things about radios that used gears instead of threading to connect the dials on the outside to the rest of the machine.

I'd been raised, for the most part, by my mom in a single-parent household. My dad had died from an illness seven years ago. He was a radio DJ. Not a famous one. He had a mini-FM radio station in Kichijoji, and he had a day job where he was just a normal salaryman. He'd started the mini-FM station as a hobby.

The station was just something he'd done on his own, and he didn't even have anything you could call "programs." It was mostly unimportant local information, like local news and the specials the local restaurants were running. But he would tell me with pride that his "Music for Kichijoji" show was actually kind of popular.

And so I'd taken after my dad. In an age when every other kid was on the internet, I'd gotten into radio.

The Skysensor my dad had given me was my treasure. I remember when I used to sit right outside during his broadcasts and listen on it.

I was the only regular listener he had.

I could hear his voice come out of the speaker a moment after he spoke. I always sat just close enough that if I listened carefully, I could hear his actual voice. It made me feel special, like I had my own seat to the show that no one else had.

If I ever die, I'm going to turn into a ghost DJ, and use my radio to

say, "Yuta! Come out and play!" from the spirit world. Remember that.
Make sure you keep tuning in and listening!

Dad used to always say that when he was alive.

When I was a kid, it scared me, but I believed him. I never thought I'd see the day when he actually died, though. When he died, I kept searching for his voice. But a week passed, and then a month, and then a year, and I never found it.

And then I finally understood.

The reason that Dad never spoke to me from the radio was because, in this world, there were no such things as ghosts. So then why was I still carrying this thing around with me, all these years later?

"I'm hungry. Let's have some suta-don today," I said.

"'You mean like every day?" Ryotasu asked.

"Garlic-soy suta-don with extra meat is the greatest thing in the world!"

"If you eat nothing but meat, you won't get enough nutrients, you know."

"There's nutrients in meat."

"Poya? In the Narusawa household, if you don't eat a balanced diet, they get mad at you. Buh."

Ryotasu puffed out her cheeks like a chipmunk. She was way too old to be doing that. But it was cute, so I'd allow it. From a boy's perspective, it didn't matter if she really meant it or if she was just putting on an act.

I put the Skysensor and my laptop in the case and then stood up to go.

"Master Izumin, put the bill on my tab," I said, though there wasn't going to be a bill or a tab—since I'd had nothing but water from the faucet.

I left the café and went down to the station to get my suta-don to go, and then sat down on a bench in Kichijoji Park. It was a tiny little park right behind the Kichijoji Theater. There was nothing there but a colorful slide for children and several benches.

"Why do you always come here instead of Inokashira Park?" Ryotasu asked.

"A *real* otaku always chooses the minority over the majority."

Inokashira Park just had too many people. And on a weekend like today, it was swarming with people who weren't even locals. There were families, couples, middle-aged joggers, old couples with dogs, girls sitting on benches and reading to try and show off their subculture cred, street performers, roadside stalls, drunks wasted on One Cup Ozeki in the middle of the day, kids running around screaming, and more. There were so many people around that it was impossible to sense the minute changes in the Skysensor.

But here in my home base of Kichijoji Park, it was always quiet. It was my secret hideout, you could say. There was usually nobody here but us, and today was no exception.

"So there's this Japanese-language broadcast called 'A Message from the Andes.' That's our target for today."

Once I'd finished my suta-don, I took out the Skysensor again and started to explain to Ryotasu how it worked. Well, today wasn't exactly the first time I'd tried. Ryotasu was the type of girl who just didn't listen.

"If you're able to listen to their broadcast, you can send them a listener's report. And they'll send you this super-rare QSL card. QSL cards are way rarer than trading cards, you know. Honestly, at this time of day, we should be able to hear it."

"Bwhom gwihbs ywo tewh cwaado?"

"Don't talk with your mouth full."

Ryotasu chewed her food for a while, and then swallowed. "Who gives you the card?"

"The radio station, obviously."

"Can you pick up radio all the way from the Andes?"

"Well, we're going to try and find out."

The winter sky was the color of twilight thinned with water. Compared to the noise around the station, this area was very quiet. Even Kichijoji turned into a quiet residential neighborhood once you got ten minutes away from the station.

I twiddled the Skysensor's dials as I stared vaguely at Ryotasu's heaving breasts.

I listened to the sounds of the meaningless white noise coming from the radio and the meaningless songs that Ryotasu sang as she danced around.

This might be my favorite part of the day.

It was like this place wasn't real.

Come to think of it, wasn't this where I'd first met Ryotasu?

It was on a summer's day about six months ago.

I'd been sitting on the bench alone, just like I was doing today. And then suddenly, without warning, she'd appeared on the slide.

"I'm your servant familiar, Gamotan!"

And from that day on, Ryotasu was my servant familiar. She didn't do anything particularly familiar-ish. In fact, she didn't even help with Kirikiri Basara. No enemies came for her to fight off with her Poyaya Gun.

I still hadn't quite figured out what had happened with that strange meeting.

The one thing I knew for sure was that Ryotasu was cute. She was cute and that was enough. Who cares about the rest of it? But since I'd remembered, I thought I may as well ask. I tried to make the question sound as natural as I could.

"Hey, Ryotasu. The first time we met, did you fall from the sky?"

"Shh!" It happened without warning.

Ryotasu put her finger up to her lips and looked at me sharply.

"Wh-what...?"

Ryotasu slid down the slide and ran over to the bench I was sitting on.

She knelt down right in front of the Skysensor on the bench next to me and stared right at my Zonko strap.

No, she was listening to the speaker, not staring at the strap.

The expression on her face wasn't the usual dopey smile. She looked extremely serious.

"—ordered our government to communicate to...China and the Soviet Union that Our Empire... provisions of their Joint Declaration..."

I thought I could hear the voice of a man through the noise, speaking in a detached and dispassionate tone.

I quickly grabbed the volume knob and turned it up. With my other hand, I adjusted the tuner at nanometer increments. (Okay, not really.)

The voice gradually became clearer and more understandable.

"—an ultimate collapse and obliteration of the Japanese nation... lead to the total extinction of human civilization."

"This is..."

"The Jewel Voice Broadcast," Ryotasu said.

It was the broadcast from Emperor Hirohito that had brought an end to the last war Japan had ever fought.

"But why?"

Ryotasu ignored me and suddenly stood up.

"Your radio really is amazing, Gamotan. I knew it!" She smiled and left the park, leaving me behind.

Amazing how? And what did she mean by "I knew it"?

"And why did you just leave me here?!"

The Jewel Voice Broadcast happened over fifty years ago. Why did my radio pick it up now?

I sat there at the park for another half hour, completely confused. By the time I got home, the sun had set.

The sun set early in the winter. Spring was a long way off.

"Uwah!" When I grabbed the doorknob to unlock the front door, I felt a sharp pain in my hand.

"More static electricity? Maybe it's because I got hit with the PYG today." I actually heard a crackling sound, so it must have been pretty bad. I don't know if my body just naturally built up electricity, but this happened a lot. It'd be cool if I could use it as some kind of electrical attack. Every kid wants to be able to shoot fire or electricity from their hands, and maybe I could use it to fight back against Ryotasu's PYG.

I grabbed the knob (it still stung a little) and opened the door.

"I'm home!" I shouted into the empty room. Of course, there was no answer.

I turned on the light switch, but my mom wasn't there. She was probably still at work.

Mom had gotten a job after Dad died. She was raising me all by herself. Sometimes during busy times, she would be gone when I got up in the morning and not get back until late at night.

I turned on the oil stove in the living room, shivering from the cold. I'd been talking with Ryotasu so long outside that my body felt like it was frozen solid.

"It's so cold..." I lived in a condo three minutes' walk from the Seimei Street intersection.

The red brick facade outside gave a clue to the building's age. It was thirty-five years old. Of course, there were no floor heaters, air conditioners, or anything like that.

I took my laptop out of the case and powered it on while I waited for the room to warm up. A laptop computer could be just as hot as your average pocket warmer, after all.

I suddenly remembered that Woodberrys place that Ryotasu had mentioned, and decided to look it up. I was primarily interested in how expensive it was.

"Hmm... a small is 320 yen. A medium is 390, and a double is 530 yen. That's even cheaper than a suta-don. Of course, the great thing about a suta-don is the absolutely crazy portion size. The name means 'stamina bowl,' after all."

If it was this cheap, I could take Ryotasu there, no problem. She really seemed to want it, after all. She was the rare 3D girl who actually hung out with me. I needed to treat her every once in a while. I wanted to make her happy. And I wanted to see her smile. If she was smiling at me, that made me happier than anything in the world.

Wow! I'm thinking like a normie! That's disgusting! It's making my skin crawl! But I kind of feel like a grown-up.

I rubbed my arm and decided to check out the comments on Kirikiri Basara. As the site admin, I wanted to be able to look at it at least five times a day. On school days, I often didn't get the chance, though.

"All right, did I get some more comments?" Like always, I started by checking the top comments on the most recent article.

"Sarai...hasn't commented yet, huh? Slacker." As I mumbled to myself, I saw a comment from an IP address that I didn't recognize.

Check Out This Super-Sexy Genius Fortune-Teller with a 99% Accuracy Rate!!
http://live.nicovideo.jp/watch/lv13448XXXX?ref=rtrec&zroute=recent &tab=live&sort=view_counter&order=desc&tags=

"Did he say...Super-Sexy?" It had nothing to do with the article, but I was still interested. Kirikiri Basara sometimes dealt with light occult stuff like fortune-telling, right?

"No, no, wait. Wait. Don't be fooled. How many times have you seen the words 'super-sexy' on the internet? She's just an amateur. Compared to an idol or an actress, let alone a 2D character, she probably isn't that great. The bar for 'super-sexy' is really high." I had to be careful.

And there was a good chance that the link might lead to something nasty. It could just be a spam link to a porn site too.

"Wait a second. Isn't this address..."

It was an address that I recognized.

This was a link to a Niconico livestream. Every NEET knew about those. Hell, even people who weren't NEETs knew.

"Hmm... It's suspicious. It's extremely suspicious. I feel like if I click on this, I'll be admitting defeat."

But...if she really *was* super-sexy, it would be a good article for Kirikiri Basara.

What to do?

"Well, whatever. I've got anti-virus installed. A free one, though." I decided to give it a click.

Actually, I was really excited to discover where it led. *Super-Sexy Genius Fortune-Teller, here I come!*

When I clicked on the link, the familiar layout of a Niconico livestream appeared on my screen.

Let's see...what's the name?

"Myu's Niconico Live Fortune-Telling. ☆" Was Myu the streamer's name?

"Oh, looks like it's just about to start."

The screen had just switched to a live camera.

It was a dimly lit room with the back wall covered in a black curtain.

A girl came into the frame from the left and sat down in a chair in front of the camera. The screen showed her from the chest up.

She looked to be about my age, maybe? She was pretty cute. She was wearing a combination of a hoodie and a blazer. It made her look like a modern fortune-teller.

She smiled a little and waved at me—that is, at the camera.

"Sometimes I'm right and sometimes I'm wrong! Believe and be saved! Or maybe not?" She spoke in a high-pitched voice like an anime character.

Her eyes narrowed on the other side of the screen. And then—

My heart skipped a beat as her voice became a hushed whisper.

"Show me your vision."

The light shone down from several directions. It had been carefully adjusted to not be too bright, but there was nothing they could do about the heat.

I sat in a corner of an elaborately decorated set, feeling the sweltering heat as I quietly began to speak.

"To scientifically prove the existence of ghosts!"

A TV studio is a very special space. It's a world of dreams, but also a world of fakery. It's both of these things at the same time.

All you had to do was look in a slightly different direction, and you'd see a whole different world. The boundaries were clearly drawn.

There was a huge difference in the world you saw looking in on the set and the world you saw looking out. That difference sometimes felt deep and profound.

"Will it make me the greatest fool of the century or will I become a 21st-century Galileo?"

A whole row of celebrities, fellow university professors, and psychics were listening to me.

"Either way, I think it's a scientist's duty to give it a try."

I'd been spending a lot more time on TV over the past year. It had all started when they'd asked me to do a little commentary about the supernatural on a variety show. The viewers seemed to have taken a liking to me, and ever since then, I'd been asked to appear on a lot of different programs.

As long as it didn't interfere with my real work as a college professor, I never turned them down. Part of me loved the attention. And so far, my personal theories had been quite well received on almost all of the programs. It felt good to be able to talk about whatever I wanted to such a large audience.

But this program today was different.

The topic was "A Heated Debate About Supernatural Phenomena." But...

"Dr. Isayuki Hashigami is a man motivated by only the highest of ideals!"

The male announcer, a man famous for his stern and severe personality, glanced down at his script. "Dr. Hashigami, I'm told you're the only official member of the SPR, or Society for Psychical Research, in Japan, yes?"

"That's correct."

"Can you tell us a little about the SPR?"

"It's an organization devoted to promoting scientific investigation into spiritual and supernatural phenomena, you see. It was founded in 1882, at Trinity College in the University of Cambridge, which makes it over a hundred years old. Several of its members are Nobel Prize winners. Jung, Freud, and Lewis Caroll were all members as well."

The guests gave a small gasp of amazement. It was understandable. The organization was completely unknown in Japan.

"For example, they're researching direct mind-to-mind communication. Some of you might know this by the name 'telepathy.' They also do research into hypnosis, spirit mediums, ghosts, spirit summoning, and the history of spiritual phenomena."

Mr. Sawazaki, who was sitting to my left side, interrupted me. "Any scientist will tell you that the SPR has a long and distinguished history in their field. However..."

I'd been told about Mr. Sawazaki before the program aired. He was a scientific fundamentalist, you could say. He appeared on these programs often, just like I did. Today was my first time meeting him.

"However, the SPR's golden age was over a hundred years ago. Is it correct to say that in the scientifically advanced era of the 21st century, they're now considered heretics?"

I chuckled a little at his accusation.

"You may be right. The stance of every member of the SPR, including myself, is that the occult can and should be proven by the scientific method. But what you have to understand is that many scientists outside Japan are seriously pursuing this research."

"That's true, but it's also a fact that there is not a single university in Japan that offers courses on parapsychology."

I nodded in agreement.

"For example, the souls of the dead do not physically exist. Science has denied their existence for centuries. And this history of denial is what modern science is built on. Am I wrong, Dr. Hashigami?" He chuckled, as if he were mocking me.

"Is that really true?" I decided to argue with him. The studio seemed to be expecting us both to lay out our positions.

"There is no proof of the nonexistence of the soul. Personally, I'm sick of science sweeping things it can't explain under the rug." I looked out over the rest of the panelists and took special note of the position of the camera as I spoke.

"Listen to me, everyone. The soul *does* exist."

A murmur went up within the studio. The off-camera staff were whispering in loud, deliberate tones.

Very few shows these days were filmed in front of a studio audience. The only ones that did were in Kansai.

"Mmmm… Spiritual!" One of the guests, a young celebrity named Mako Utsumi, whispered like she was drunk.

The off-camera staff gave a loud burst of laughter.

Utsumi was a popular talent on these sorts of programs lately. She had the composed looks of a model but her comments were funnier than those of most comedians. TV stations loved her.

The announcer decided to move the conversation to her.

"Miss Utsumi, what's your take on this?"

"I don't really know but Dr. Hashigami sure is handsome, isn't he? How do you take care of that long hair of yours? It goes all the way down to your waist. Most girls don't even have hair that long. I'd love to hear how you take care of it. I can practically see your cuticles!"

The staff burst out laughing again.

"That's Utsumi for you. She always has the most unique comments. Very unique. But we're not really talking about cuticles right now, okay?" The announcer tried to bring things back on topic.

Mr. Sawazaki leaned toward me to continue. "So you say the soul exists, Dr. Hashigami? So, what, do our souls leave our bodies after death? If you're saying they do, then what you're describing is no different than an old ghost story."

Mr. Sawazaki's tone had become heated. He was much less calm than he'd been a moment ago.

I tried to answer his question as calmly as I could. "The soul stays within the brain while a person is alive, but after their heart stops, it is ejected from the body."

"No, no, no. That's not an answer. Let me guess. You have no scientific proof of this, do you? That's how it always is with you parapsychology types. If you're going to just make claims without evidence, then you should just start off by admitting you're no different than a fortune-teller. And you know something, Dr. Hashigami? I've never liked the way you keep coming up with all these theories that have no scientific backing whatsoever." He was spoiling for a fight.

The other guests looked slightly confused. None of them were capable of intervening.

"In the end, everything you're saying only exists in your own head. If you keep this up, you're liable to discredit the entire field of parapsychology, you know. Parapsychology is still a new field of study, and it's trying its best to find scientific evidence for its claims, but it still hasn't left the realm of the occult. Of course, I'll admit there's value in such research, but I think you need another half century of real, solid, experimentally proven results. And yet you, Dr. Hashigami, come on these TV shows and say things for which you have not the slightest evidence. It's deplorable. Simply deplorable!"

Mr. Sawazaki seemed to think he was lecturing me. "Or what, are you going to tell me you've found scientific evidence for these claims? Then I'll ask why you haven't submitted them to the rest of the scientific community. Your individual claim that the soul exists does not suffice as objective proof. That's why I say you're the same as a fortune-teller. What do you have to say to that?"

For a moment, I thought about telling him everything. But I held back the urge.

"Unfortunately, there are good reasons why I can't publish yet. Scientifically speaking, however, ghosts do exist. What you and the others call the 'occult' is just a caricature."

"But that's not an argument! You say you've got reasons? What are your reasons, then?"

"..." Suddenly, I remembered something.

My young son had once told me the same things that Sawazaki had just said.

My son was a college student now. He was my only child and I loved him as much as I loved myself. I loved him so much that I took him everywhere when he was young. Sometimes, I'd even bring him to academic conferences or lectures. I didn't know if that was the reason, but from a young age, he'd been one of those rare boys to take an interest in science. But when I'd become an official member of the SPR—about five years ago—he'd asked me a question.

"Dad, do you just want attention, or do you really want scientific proof that the spirit world is real?"

That was when I'd realized that at some point, a deep rift had developed between me and my son.

My son was a dedicated perfectionist, and a denier of the occult, just like Mr. Sawazaki.

"There are no such things as souls, and the supernatural doesn't exist. There certainly isn't a spirit world. It's impossible for the minds of the dead to float around in midair. It's just animal instincts in the human mind that make you feel that way. The occult can easily be explained by modern science. And parapsychology is too close to outright pseudoscience."

My son had been highly intelligent from a young age and ironically, his talents had led him to develop the exact opposite stance from my own research.

When he was young, though, he used to tell me all the time that he'd seen ghosts. When I pointed that out, he even analyzed his own memories as a combination of "childhood amnesia and false memories."

He really could be a stubborn brat sometimes.

By the time I'd started to appear on TV, my relationship with my son had gone past the point of no return. I would see him occasionally, and I could literally feel the disgust in his eyes. I couldn't help but notice. I was his father, after all. The son said that he could prove, scientifically, that the spirit world did not exist. And the father said that he could prove, scientifically, that it did.

These two beliefs were the exact opposite of one another.

Was there ever a father and son as ridiculous as we were? I chuckled to myself as I remembered his cold glare, despite the fact that I was on TV.

"It's the spirits of the dead! The suffering of the dead becomes a curse and stalks the earth!" My debate with Mr. Sawazaki (or more precisely, Mr. Sawazaki's one-sided berating of me) was suddenly interrupted by a strange yell to my right.

It came from a woman in her early 50s, a self-proclaimed spiritualist named Shizuko Motomura.

The announcer, however, pretended that he didn't hear her.

"Dr. Hashigami, you just said that after the heart stops, the soul is ejected from the body. Can you tell us more about what you meant? Do souls just float in the air, then?"

Before I could answer, Mrs. Motomura screamed in a voice like nails on a chalkboard. "They're wandering through this studio! Spirits bound to the earthly realm, unable to accept their deaths!"

The announcer motioned for me to continue, completely ignoring her. He seemed to be urging me to answer as soon as possible. I nodded.

"Yes, that's right. But to use more scientific terminology, they're not ghosts so much as they are electromagnetic fields."

"I'm sorry? Electromagnetic fields?"

"*Grrckk*... Ahem!"

Mrs. Motomura cleared her throat loudly but the announcer leaned forward toward me instead.

"Can you tell us more?"

"They're thought patterns that are saved in a magnetic field and protected by an electric one."

"*Hmm*... I see. That's quite an interesting theory. Well, I'll be honest. I'm having a little trouble keeping up with this. So this electromagnetic field is similar to a storage device? Like you'd find on a computer?"

"That's correct. The information is stored magnetically and protected electrically. This is the same method used in both digital and analog media." I took out a chart that I'd had the staff prepare for me in advance. It displayed a diagram of the soul according to my theory.

"After death, the information recorded in the human brain leaves the body as magnetic field data with a will of its own. This, primarily, is what is indicated with the word 'ghost.'"

"Wow, really?" Miss Utsumi's wide eyes went even wider as she gasped in surprise.

"Most all examples of spiritual phenomena can be explained by use of this electromagnetic field theory."

"It sounds kind of like plasma." Mr. Sawazaki muttered to himself. He sounded like he was sulking.

The announcer ignored him, too, as he continued to question me.

"If the occult could, in fact, be explained via the scientific method, wouldn't it cease to be occult at all?"

"No, that's not correct. As I've said in my books, we'll soon be able to completely explain spiritual phenomena with science in the near future. But that's just the beginning. That will be the first time that the occult is, in the true sense, recognized scientifically."

"*Mm*... You kind of sound like you're talking about a religion, Dr. Hashigami. I'll admit it makes for a compelling story, though." At this point I'd just stopped paying attention to Mr. Sawazaki altogether.

"You heard Dr. Sawazaki a moment ago, yes? Parapsychology is still a young field. I'm well aware that we have a long way to go. You'll remember that they mocked Copernicus's heliocentrism at first, too. So I don't think it's appropriate for Dr. Sawazaki to be so dismissive of the occult, or my own theories. Humanity should be less aggressive, and more humble, about its own ignorance. The newest discoveries await us not in space but very close to us. And I'm sure those discoveries will bring us all a great deal of joy."

"That's what I mean when I say it sounds like a religion. Explain to me what separates you from that crazy old fraud of a spiritualist over the—" He cut off mid-sentence.

Miss Utsumi had suddenly put her hands to her chest and doubled over in pain.

"*Aah... ahh...*" She was moaning as if she was in agony and her face looked extremely pale. There were beads of sweat forming on her forehead.

"Miss Utsumi? What's wrong?" The announcer sounded worried.

Was she sick?

It felt like someone should go over to help her, but since this was a live broadcast, no one was sure what to do.

I could see the staff starting to panic in the background. But the man who seemed to be the director was just waving his arms around instead of giving clear orders.

"Begone!" Amidst the chaos, there was one person that stayed calm.

Mrs. Motomura shouted, spittle flicking from her mouth, as she looked around the studio.

Shrine priestesses dressed in white ceremonial clothing ran onto the stage. The camera was still running, but they didn't care. There was no explanation as to who they were.

"This room is filled with the spirits of evil! And this girl, too!" Mrs. Motomura pointed at Miss Utsumi, who still seemed to be in pain.

"She is being possessed by evil, earthbound spirits!" One of the priestesses took an onusa, a wooden wand used in Shinto rituals, and handed it to Mrs. Motomura.

She and the others must have been Mrs. Motomura's students or something.

She brought down the onusa again and again on top of Miss Utsumi.

"Uweh! Keih! Sweyh!"

No one else could do anything but look on in shock. For some reason, despite all this, the cameras were still rolling.

"Evil spirits, begone from this mortal vessel! *Keih!*"

"*Gwa... gwaaaaahhh!*" Miss Utsumi screamed in a voice that didn't sound anything like what I'd heard from her earlier. Drool was dripping from her mouth and her eyes had rolled back in her head.

Only then did one of the staff members come out with instructions written on a whiteboard.

"Cut to commercial!" it said. The announcer nodded.

"I'm sorry. We'll be back after these messages."

After a few seconds, someone in the back yelled, "Commercials are rolling!" Then several of the staff carried Miss Utsumi out of the studio.

Mrs. Motomura gave a sigh of satisfaction and went back to her seat.

"That was a close call" was all she whispered before she sent her students out of the room.

"..." It felt like everything I'd just seen had happened in some faraway world. It didn't seem like there'd be any way we could hold a real debate now.

When the commercials ended, the program continued without Utsumi.

The announcer spoke to Mrs. Motomura.

"So, Mrs. Motomura, is Miss Utsumi going to be all right?"

"The spirits have left. She'll be fine. You should know that your words have angered the spirits and brought this upon her." Evidently, she was trying to say that it was Mr. Sawazaki's and my fault.

I didn't really care but Mr. Sawazaki overreacted.

"That's stupid. It's simply ridiculous. I've seen plenty of fake spiritualists like you, who want to make a business out of the occult." Just like before, he was making no attempt to hide his irritation. But now his anger was directed at Mrs. Motomura, not me.

Mrs. Motomura's eyes went wide as she shouted back. "Fools like you are the first to die—and not only that, but you'll die quaking in fear!" There was no way to recover from that.

I couldn't believe they were getting so excited over a debate on a TV program.

Didn't they realize how many millions of people were watching? They were essentially embarrassing themselves in front of every single one of them. If you were incapable of debating in a calm, controlled manner, you had no business being on TV in the first place. But what I really couldn't believe was that neither the announcer nor the staff were trying to stop this. It was like they'd given up on any attempt at making this program work.

And what was most unbelievable of all was that the announcer calmly brought the program to its end.

"I'm sure we all have a lot more to talk about, but unfortunately, we're all out of time. This concludes this evening's episode of *Psychic Research Lab: Special Edition*. Thanks for tuning in."

Since it was a live broadcast, when the time slot was over, they had to end it. Still, I'd never heard of a program ending like this. They were going to be swamped with complaints from viewers, right?

"Dr. Hashigami, do you have any last words for us?"

And now they were coming to me to end it. I could still see Mr. Sawazaki and Mrs. Motomura glaring at each other on either side of me.

I sighed. "I'll pass on saying anything about that little fracas back there, but I do want to say something about Dr. Sawazaki's comments. Dr. Sawazaki believes that a scientist should refuse to accept the existence of anything beyond the physical. I disagree. The reason that Japan lags behind so much in parapsychology research is that our scientists, and Japanese people in particular, all seem to share in this sort of one-sided belief." Mr. Sawazaki was so busy glaring at Mrs. Motomura that he didn't even seem to notice what I'd said.

"I'd like to thank all of our panelists for coming." The announcer bowed and the program ended.

"And that's a wrap! Great work, everyone!" The program's producer, Mr. Nozaki, came over to us.

"Thanks for coming, Dr. Hashigami."

"Thank you for inviting me. But is Miss Utsumi all right?"

"Huh? Oh, Utsumi, yeah. Look over there." Mr. Nozaki nodded in the direction of the studio's entrance.

I looked over and saw that Utsumi was standing there like nothing had happened. She was smiling at the staff.

"Oh, Nozaki!" She waved and came over.

"Utsumi, that was great back there. I bet you could make it as an actress."

"Aw, Nozaki. You're so silly." It was a strange conversation.

It was like the pain she'd been suffering was just an act.

Then Mr. Nozaki smiled and shouted across the room to Mrs. Motomura.

"You did great too, Motomura! We're going to put on another special in summer! Can you give us something even more flashy?"

"You're what keeps us in business, Nozaki. Of course, we'll be glad to help. Come on, you guys. Say thank you."

Mrs. Motomura forced the students around her to turn toward Mr. Nozaki and bow.

Just a moment ago, she'd been glaring daggers at Mr. Sawazaki, but the minute the program finished, she transformed into a kindly old woman. The expression on her face had relaxed as well.

"We don't have the ratings yet but the response on the internet looks really positive. My years of intuition tell me that we're likely to break 20%. You don't see these sorts of incidents or really heated debates on TV these days. I think viewers will find it a nice change of pace, you know?" Mr. Nozaki was in a great mood.

Finally, he smiled and exchanged a firm handshake with Mr. Sawazaki as well.

"Mr. Nozaki, I'll be heading out."

"Thank you, Sawazaki. You should relax a little and come back and see us more often! You're the only one who can do what you do, and lately you're really starting to develop your own unique character. You were amazing today! If you keep it up, I promise I'll make you a regular."

"I'll do my best," he laughed. Mr. Sawazaki had become a different person the second the program ended as well.

"Man, that was really harsh at the end, though. What was it? A fake spiritualist who wants to make a business out of the occult? The way you yelled was perfect! Though I have to admit, when I heard it I said to myself, 'That goes for you, too!'"

"It was a good script. Thank the person who wrote it. I'm actually a real gentleman, you see. Fwahaha!"

I sighed a little as I listened to them. The whole thing was a farce, from start to finish. Not a single person in this studio except me was serious about the spirit world. That's why no one had tried to stop the argument when it had gone off the rails.

Was this just what television was like? I was starting to make a bit of a name for myself in this business but maybe it was time to say goodbye.

I went back to my dressing room to get my things together, then left the TV station.

It was about a minute's walk from the recording studio to the private parking lot. It was already pretty late and the narrow corridor to the parking lot was dark and gloomy. There was no one else here. The LED lighting buried into the ground lit up the sides of the path.

A dark silhouette suddenly rose up in front of me in the center of the lit path.

I looked closer, thinking it might be a ghost. But it wasn't. The silhouette became clearer as it began to approach me.

It wasn't a ghost. It was a living human being.

They were wearing a white cape. It was one of the people I'd been on the program with just a moment ago.

Mrs. Motomura was standing in front of me, blocking the path.

I knew she could hear my footsteps, but she didn't say anything.

"Good work today, Mrs. Motomura." I tried to be as casual as possible as I spoke to her.

Then suddenly, she opened her eyes wide and looked at me.

Her face twisted into something terrible, like a scream of terror. I froze.

"..." She said nothing.

She glared at me, eyes wide, saying nothing at all.

It was a far more imposing sight than when she'd been screaming at the studio earlier. The aura surrounding her was totally different.

I wasn't sure what to do.

What was she doing there? Why was she blocking me?

Had she been waiting for me here? Was she here to complain about something I'd said on the program?

If she was, she'd probably do better to complain to Mr. Sawazaki instead of me. He was the one who'd been shouting at her.

If I wanted to get to the parking lot, I had to go past her. It would be rude to just turn around and leave.

Seeing no other option, I started to walk forward, trying my best to act casual. She kept looking at me with that mad expression. She was definitely following me with her eyes. But she still wasn't saying a word.

I bowed a little and tried to pass her.

And then I thought to myself, *Is Mrs. Motomura going to try and kill me?*

"That's right." The whisper in my ear wasn't the high-pitched voice I'd heard in the studio. It was a low growl, like a man's.

▶ site 03: Aria Kurenaino ——— 2/11 (Thursday)

In the quiet room, each time I moved my hands, I heard the sound of rustling silk.

Whenever I was waiting for a customer, I always spent my time sewing dolls. They were actually stuffed animals but I called them dolls.

I cut out the fabric according to the pattern and sewed it together. There were already almost a hundred of these homemade dolls scattered around my house. It was possible I spent more time sewing here in the shop than doing anything else. I was lucky, after all, if I got a single customer in a day.

This was my shop.

It was tiny, less than three meters per side, and the shelves and table took up most of the space. It could fit three adults at the absolute maximum.

The ceiling was low, too. I wasn't a tall person myself but I felt cramped when I stood up.

The windows were sealed shut and covered with black cloth.

The only light in the room was a single bare bulb hanging from the ceiling. Even though the sun was high in the sky, it was still dark and gloomy.

I poured myself a cup of herbal tea from my teapot and took a sip. The warmth from the tea soaked into my chest. I sighed a little as I wrapped my freezing hands around the cup to warm them.

The building wasn't particularly well built, so, of course, it was drafty. This room didn't have any kind of heater, so this time of year, hot tea was all that kept me warm.

I could faintly hear the hustle and bustle outside. I liked to listen quietly to the sounds.

It was a shopping area in front of Kichijoji Station called Harmonica Alley, narrow little streets packed tight with shops. There was only barely enough room for a person to fit between the stores in the alleyways.

It had gotten its start as a black market after World War II and there were still traces of that today. There were bars, cafés, fishmongers, general stores, florists...a random hodgepodge of anything you could imagine.

Over the past few years, people had even built some bright, inviting, and fashionable stores, too. During the day, there were a lot of girls here.

At night, the shutters went up on the places that served alcohol, and men stopped by on their way home from work. Of course, that was true of bars in any town.

But most people passed by my store, whether it was day or night. Even with all the different shops in Harmonica Alley, mine was clearly unique.

The sign out front—it was closer in size to a plaque—read, "Black Magic Agency—The House of Crimson." If anyone saw that plaque and came inside, they were clearly a little unique themselves.

Suddenly I heard faint footsteps on the stairs below.

That was enough for me to realize that tonight, my strange little shop would actually have a customer. And it was a woman, too. Just by listening, I could hear the sound of high heels. She was cautious as she walked, but that was true of everyone who came here.

The shop was on the second floor of the building. Anyone who came would have to go up a cramped, steep staircase.

I could sense someone outside the door.

Slowly, it opened. One of the hinges had almost fallen off, so it made a high-pitched creaking noise, like the cry of a bat.

A woman in her thirties peeked in. Her face looked pale.

"Um... This is the black magic agency, yes?"

"Welcome to the House of Crimson. Please be seated."

The woman bowed to me and came inside.

She didn't seem to be feeling well, and she was covering her mouth with a handkerchief. And she was shaking, whether it was from the cold or for some other reason.

She swayed a little as she sat down in the rococo-style chair across from me.

She didn't even try to hide the way she was staring at me.

"So you're...Aria Kurenaino? You're quite young."

"..." I put away the doll I was sewing and returned her bow.

I heard that a lot.

My age, my appearance...this shop had nothing to do with worldly things like that. That's why I had no intention of talking about them

myself.

"I didn't know where this place was, so I wandered around Harmonica Alley a long time. I'd say about twenty minutes." She tried to force herself to smile. But it didn't work, and she ended up with a strange, twisted expression.

"The entrance to this place smells so bad though, doesn't it? Is there a garbage pickup spot nearby? I think there's a lot of bars and eateries around here."

I ignored her comments and poured her a new cup of tea.

I didn't talk about things that didn't matter. I didn't feel the need. They didn't want me to, either. Especially the sort of person who came to this shop.

"It's your first time here, correct?"

I offered her the cup of tea to warm her up, but she didn't take a sip. Instead, she looked at me, searchingly.

"Yes, that's right. It's...in rather bad taste, isn't it?"

Some people seemed to think that, yes. Her eyes were terribly cloudy as she spoke.

No, it wasn't just her eyes.

I hadn't noticed at first because of the dim light from the exposed bulb, but now that I saw her in front of me, I could tell.

Her skin was a mess, and her hair was unkempt, too. Her coat was battered and in poor condition.

She seemed to be brooding over something, hard.

"I was told that you can place curses on other people here at this store," she said. That's right. I was a professional black magic agent.

Any time two human beings interacted, one person was sure to hate the other. Those negative emotions would never disappear, not even decades or centuries from now.

But the risk of carrying out black magic was too great, and it took knowledge and skill as well. So I would practice black magic on other people's behalf.

That was my job as a black magic executor.

"Tell me your story." I took a candelabra from the shelf next to me and put it on the table. It had two black candles in it. I struck a match and lit them. Then I turned off the light.

The room grew darker.

Our shadows flickered against the wall in the candlelight.

It was easier for people to talk in the darkness. Especially if they were saying something that made them feel guilty. Creating such a space made communications with the client go more smoothly.

The curtain had already risen on the stage. I was what my customer sought, the jester known as a "black magician."

And now, I will dance for you...

So show me your darkness.

I smiled to relax her, and the woman leaned forward.

"I want you to kill a certain man." Her tone, naturally, dropped.

That was a very common request. I'd taken many such jobs in the past, so I didn't find it surprising at all.

"Black magic requires the use of a catalyst. Have you brought such an object with you today?"

The woman nodded slowly, and then took an envelope out of her bag.

There was no name on the envelope, but inside was a carefully folded piece of paper.

She put it on the table and spread it out.

"I see." Inside was a lock of hair. It was about five centimeters long. There were ten or so strands.

Without the hair of the person I was cursing, I refused to accept a job. But if they brought the hair, I never turned them down, no matter who they were or who they wanted to curse.

I handed the woman a blank white sheet of paper. Then I dipped a black feather pen into ink mixed with bat's blood and put it in her hand.

"Would you please give me more information about the person you wish to curse? Name, height, weight, birthday, blood type, address, family members' names, school name, company name...the more information, the more likely it will succeed."

The customer nodded and began to fill out the page, her eyes bloodshot.

She was writing a lot of detail, enough that she had to dip her pen in the inkwell many times.

I prepared the censer as she wrote. I heated a piece of charcoal in the candle's flame, then placed it on top of the censer's grating. Then I slowly shook a black powder incense made from citronella grass and wisteria on top of it.

The shop was filled with its unique scent.

"Will this be...enough?"

"Yes. That's plenty." By the time she was done, she'd filled the whole piece of paper. From the amount of information she put down, the man she was cursing was either an ex-husband or a former lover.

But I had no interest in asking for more details.

In my role as an agent, the relationship between the client and the target was not a matter of particular importance.

I folded up the paper and put it into a small, clear bottle. A cloth had already been spread out on the table. I put the bottle at the center of the triquetra pattern on the cloth.

"I'll explain the packages we offer, then."

"P-packages?"

"The House of Crimson offers three packages for you to choose from. The number of dolls used in the incantation changes depending on the package you pick."

"Dolls?"

"Think of them as servant familiars, if you like."

The client seemed confused.

I pointed to the dolls on the shelves behind me. They were my familiars, which I had made myself.

"The most affordable curse is the Tomorrow of Despair package, priced at 9,999 yen. With this package, I will use one doll."

I took a doll from the shelf and put it on the edge of the triquetra.

It was Ahriman, a doll with a green striped body and bug eyes.

"The mid-range option is the Dying Screams package. It goes for 42,420 yen." I took two more dolls off the shelf and put them on the table.

Gorgon had a honeybee-striped body and the face of a dog.

Coven had five eyes and a body patterned with stars.

"The first-class package is the Devil's Ritual. This package goes for 66,600 yen." I took one of the last two dolls—Peter, a mouse with a bright purple body and multicolored fabric teeth—and put him to the side of the bottle.

Then I took Lilith XII, a black cat prince who'd lost his tail and whose head was covered in a burlap sack to hide his face, and put him at the top of the pentagram.

"Which would you like today?"

The woman hesitated before she spoke.

"I'll take the cheapest one..." She seemed reluctant as she whispered.

It seemed like she didn't have the money for the others.

Her hatred for her enemy wasn't enough to overcome her financial difficulties. It was sad but that was the way of the world.

"The Tomorrow of Despair package, yes?"

I returned the other four dolls to the shelf and left Ahriman on the table.

"I will now begin the ritual."

"The ritual..."

"It's part of the process in performing black magic. It's possible, strictly speaking, for the spell to succeed without a ritual, however. What's most important is the strength of your will. But you want to really feel like you've put a curse on him, don't you?"

"Y-you're right."

"And this is a step in that process."

This ritual was old but I'd added my own touches to it.

Black magic amplifies a person's negative emotions, so skipping steps in the ritual could cause the curse to affect those around you.

So by adding my own modifications to the ritual, I had lessened the amount of negative power in play. I reverently lifted up a dagger in both hands and offered it to the client.

"I'll take a few drops of your blood. Will you prick your finger for me? Either hand is fine."

The client did as she was told and pricked her left index finger with the dagger. A tiny bit of blood came out from the small wound.

I gently took her finger and led it to the bottle on the table.

The blood dripped down into the bottle and made a red stain on the paper.

"Yes, that will do." I gently wiped her finger with a tissue.

I put the cork in the bottle to seal it.

Then I put Ahriman right next to it.

I picked up the hair the client had brought with a pair of tweezers.

"I will now burn the catalyst. As I do so, chant the most awful curses you can imagine in your heart." The client nodded.

I brought the hair close to the black candles.

There was a stench and a crackle as the hair began to burn.

The client stared at it, unblinking, as if she was possessed by something.

When all the hair was burnt, I blew out the black candles.

The shop became totally black.

"The ritual is complete. Thank you. If your will is strong enough, the curse will succeed."

Which meant, of course, that if her will was weak, the curse would fail.

I never told any of my clients that the curse was certain to succeed.

I turned on the lights and received my payment.

The client smiled slightly, satisfied, and left the shop.

"A woman's story is always a sad thing, isn't it?" I took the cork off the bottle on the table, then took out the paper inside and carefully moved it to a small box.

I had no intention of looking at the information about the target myself. I wasn't the one who placed the curse. I was simply an agent. The work was done by a devil.

I put away the customer's untouched cup of tea, and then took out my tablet PC from the drawer in the table.

It didn't really go well with the gothic feel of the shop, so I probably shouldn't have been using it so much. But since I received so few customers, lately, I'd stopped caring.

I touched the tablet to bring up my email app. The House of Crimson had a homepage and that was actually where I interacted with most potential clients. I made sure to check it at least once a day.

Just as I thought, I had a message waiting for me.

The title was straightforward: "Request for Black Magic Execution."

My policy was to just glance through request emails, and most of the time, to discard them. Hardly any of them ever paid.

The homepage said that clients were required to visit my shop in person, but sometimes, I got messages like this anyway.

Today's email came with an image attached.

I looked at the sender's name before I opened it.

"Fukuzo...Moguro?"

Even I knew who that was and I wasn't exactly up-to-date on popular culture. It was a character from a decades-old manga.

This was clearly a false name. Either they didn't want me to know their real name or they were simply playing a prank. There were actually a lot of people who didn't like shops like mine and would play tricks like this. That was probably all this email was.

The message text was just a single line.

"Death."

Very simple. And thus, very easy to understand. I liked that.

I decided to open the attached image.

When I opened it, I bit down hard on my back teeth without even realizing it.

The cold temperature in the room seemed to drop another few degrees.

It was an upside-down pentagram drawn in bright red lines. The inversion made it a demonic symbol. And in the center of the pentagram were letters drawn by hand.

"〒666 Isayuki Hashigami." I knew that name, too.

It was a scientist who'd been all over the TV and magazines lately. He was a middle-aged gentleman, with distinctive long hair that went down to his waist. Despite his age, his black hair was beautiful and lustrous, and it left a strong impression even on a girl like me.

His job was to introduce the media to all kinds of different occult ideas. What made him interesting was that despite his role as a scientist, he was a believer in the occult, who said that he could scientifically prove the existence of ghosts.

The public had started to pick up on his existence and the media was having its first occult programming boom in a long while because of him. He was popular enough that there were probably a lot of people who wanted to see him dead.

How disgusting.

That was my first thought as a person who called herself a black magician.

I could feel a strong aura of hate in these rough, hand-written letters, the kind of thing that was difficult to discern via digital text.

It was easy to extract their meaning.

"666 is the number of the Devil...or perhaps, the cost of his chosen package?" The number 666 appeared in the Bible, and it had been used as the number of the Devil since ancient times.

The House of Crimson used it as well. The most expensive black magic I offered was the Devil's Ritual and its cost was 66,6000 yen. It was written on the homepage as well.

But what was 〒?

"The postal mark." The mailbox for this shop was downstairs. Had someone left something there? I wasn't able to hear the footsteps from that far away.

But then what had they left?

Money? Or something else?

The awful premonition I felt kept growing stronger. It was like a ghost was licking the crook of my neck. It was extremely unpleasant.

I stood up from my chair, shivering from the cold. If something was in my mailbox, I couldn't just leave it there.

I opened the door, which led directly to a series of steep steps.

I grimaced. There was the strong smell of something rotten. I remembered the last customer talking about a terrible smell. Maybe that was why she had the handkerchief to her face.

I'd arrived here shortly before noon. No one had visited the shop until her.

Had someone been here during that time? From upstairs, the mailbox looked like it was filled with something black. It definitely wasn't a package. It was something much worse.

I slowly walked down the narrow stairs, taking care not to trip.

The smell almost made me vomit. I put my hand over my mouth but it didn't make a difference at all.

I somehow made it to the bottom and out into the street.

The tiny street where I had my shop was off of the main area. Most of the shops around it were bars, and since the sun hadn't set yet, their shutters were still down. That meant there was no one here.

Just a few meters away, I could hear the bustle of a busy street, but...

It felt like I had wandered into a tiny portal to hell that had just opened near Kichijoji Station.

I gulped and turned to face the mailbox. Even from the outside I could see that it was stuffed tightly with something black.

I opened it up, trying my best not to vomit. The handle was slick with some kind of liquid. It was dark black—blood.

When I opened the mailbox, the stuff inside spilled to the ground.

It was a lump, like vomit, but different. It was the size of a soccer ball and soft. It was...

"Human...hair."

The ball of hair was wet with black blood and glistened in the light.

There so much of it. If all of this came from one person, he must have had very long hair.

I grabbed the ends with my bare hands and picked them up.

And then I realized...

It wasn't just hair.

The hair was growing out of what looked like the mesh frame of a wig. The frame was the color of skin on one side, but on the other side it was slick and pink.

It was human flesh.

This wasn't a wig.

Which meant it could only be one thing.

All this hair belonged to one person, and someone had ripped off their scalp.

I immediately thought of someone with long hair.

Professor Hashigami.

I could feel the depth of the hatred possessed by the person who had left this here and I was confused.

If they were capable of ripping off the professor's scalp, then why did "Fukuzo Moguro" need me to put a curse on him?

But there was one thing I did know.

This was a job. The hair I needed for the catalyst was proof of that.

My knees started to shake as I thought about it. I sat down on the stairs, cradling the ball of hair with both hands.

"What a terrible obsession...it makes me want to throw up."

PARANORMAL SCIENCE NVL

Occultic;Nine

THERE IS NO SUCH THING AS THE "OCCULT." IT CAN ALL BE DISPROVED BY SCIENCE.
ONLY THOSE WHO HAVE ACCEPTED EVERYTHING
HAVE THE RIGHT TO KNOW THE TRUTH.

"Show me your vision."

It felt kind of like telling someone you loved them. That's what I always thought. The tiny, whispered message I always spoke to start my streams was kind of like a love letter to someone I'd never met.

I looked at the laptop in front of me. It was showing the page for the program I was broadcasting. The screen was filled with comments from viewers, flowing from right to left.

"Glad to have you back!"

"Myu, you're so cute!"

"Tell me your real name!"

"Are you a real fortune-teller?"

"Looking forward to today's stream!"

"She's a fake."

"That voice is so hot."

"Oh, she's a slut, huh?"

I almost sighed aloud when I saw them but stopped myself. "Right, right. Stop messing around. And who the heck calls someone

a slut just over seeing their face?"

"Myu! You forgot your introduction!"

I could see my friend Chi in the corner of the room, frantically scribbling on a whiteboard. She was my best friend and she always helped me with the show. It was actually her idea to do it in the first place.

I switched gears and pulled the hood up over my head. I adjusted my bangs a little and winked toward the camera inside my laptop. The image of me on the screen winked as well.

"Hi there. Hello to all you first-timers, and to the rest of you, how was your week? I'm Myu, your host. Thanks for coming to see today's 'Myu's Niconico Live Fortune-Telling'! I'm so happy you did. Since you're here, have some fun!"

Myu was my name on the show. Of course, it wasn't my real name. My real name was Miyuu Aikawa. But I thought it was a pretty cute nickname. I actually really liked it now. Maybe I owed Chi, since she came up with it.

I took a quick look at the number of viewers. Whoa...already over 10,000. I'd only been in front of the camera for a minute or two!

It was kind of creepy when I thought about how most of them were men, though. About 90% of my show's viewers were men, which was pretty unusual for a fortune-telling stream. It was even scarier to think that by the time it reached 50,000, I'd basically be doing my fortune-telling in front of a packed house at the Tokyo Dome. Best not to think about it too much.

I'd started doing this stream at home after Chi had gotten the idea and dragged me into it. But I'd ended up being really popular, and the first time my viewer count hit 50,000, I'd gotten a message from Niconico's staff. After that, they promoted me, and my stream became official. Isn't that nuts? I find it a little hard to believe myself but it's all true.

More comments came after I finished my introduction.

"You're so cute, Myu! So cute!"

"Wow, this girl is so cute!"

"She's looking cute again today."

"I want to lick her."

"Her voice is so hawt."

"I want to lick her hair."

"I want to lick her neck."

"I want to lick her eyeballs."

"I want to lick her ear canal."

"Guys, shut up with the licking, lol."

"Don't lick me, my little puppies! It's super-creepy!" I chuckled.

More comments came back, and they were even creepier this time.

"I love a tsundere!"

"I'll lick you more!"

"I want to lick inside your nostrils!"

"I'm fine with being creepy!"

"Thank you for the cold stare."

"Insult me more!"

"*Uhh*, I'll delete any more creepy comments, okay. Seriously, I'll show no mercy!"

I didn't really like putting up with stuff like this. I just wanted to focus on testing my fortune-telling power.

Well, I didn't really *mind* all the attention. But lately, there'd been nothing but noise in the comments. That made it impossible to focus on my fortune-telling, so it was pretty stressful. Not that there was any point in complaining, I guess.

I slapped my cheeks to help myself focus. "All right, are you ready for some fortune-telling? Oh, but should I tell you a little about this program first?"

The plan was to just say what I wanted to say in as cheerful a manner as I could say it. That way, when it was all over, I could just forget it. That was the policy I'd decided on with Chi and I was going to stick to that decision.

"Okay, first, a quick explanation. This program stars me, the self-proclaimed fortune-teller, Myu. I've decided to call all you viewers my 'little lost puppies,' so keep that in mind. And I've got a revolutionary way for you puppies to get in contact with me. Just call me on my phone! Who will be chosen? Only fate can tell you!"

Of course, this wasn't my personal phone. It was just a number I used for the show. I had two cellphones now. During the first episode, I'd used my real number, but Chi had told me that it was dangerous.

"So is everybody ready? Here's the number!"

I typed the phone number in with my keyboard, and then turned on the phone.

A moment later, it showed up in the special streamer comment box on the screen.

At the exact same moment, the phone began to ring.

"Wow, you guys are too fast." But the call quickly stopped and went to voice mail. This was deliberate.

I had the phone set to go directly to voice mail after three rings. During those three rings, I'd decide if I would pick it up or not. I didn't really have any reason why I'd answer one call and ignore another. It came down to how I felt at any given moment.

I decided to ignore the phone for a moment. Instead, I took the cards I used for fortune-telling out of my hoodie's pocket and put them onto the table. The cards were like tarot cards but a little different.

Those cards are the mirror of your heart. They are your animus.

Dad's words flashed through my mind, and I sighed, softly.

"All right, let's talk to our first little lost puppy for today!"

The calls were coming in fast. The phone would ring, then go right to voice mail, and then ring again. I looked at each number as it appeared on my caller ID and waited for the right moment to pick one.

It was important to keep the viewers a little anxious. That was something I'd learned over my past twelve broadcasts.

"Okay, I've got it! Push the button!" I pressed the button and answered the call that had just come in. I set the phone to speaker mode and started to talk.

"Hello? This is Niconico Live Fortune-Telling. You're on."

"Oh, huh? Oh, hi. Wow, I actually made it through!" I could hear an excited male voice on the other side of the phone.

"Tell me your name."

"Oh, call me Mochi-Mochi Pon-Pon. Thanks for talking to me, Myu."

"Of course. Thanks for your call." I bowed to the camera.

"All right, Mr. Mochi-Mochi Pon-Pon, tell me what I can help you with."

He wanted some help with a love interest of his.

There was a person he liked at his company, but he was sure that they weren't interested in him. It was obvious that if he asked them out, they'd hate him. But he wanted to work up the courage to do it anyway. Should he work up the courage to do it? Something like that.

It was a pretty standard request, but from the tone of his voice, I could tell that he was pretty desperate.

If he was talking about a coworker, did that mean that Mr. Mochi-Mochi Pon-Pon was out of school? Somebody like *that* was seriously asking me to help him with my fortune-telling?

Would I be able to help him?

"Okay. Time for Myu's Niconico Fortune-Telling to begin!" I shouted.

Then I picked up the stack of cards. I shuffled them, then laid them facedown on the table.

Normally fortune-tellers used the Major Arcana from a deck of tarot cards. But I was different.

I'd made these cards myself. They were all very poorly drawn. Each depicted a tiny girl and a dog with the body of a man, who I called Dogman. I'd drawn every image with crayons when I was little.

Dad had actually taken pictures of them to preserve them. And these cards were printed from those photographs.

There were twenty-two in all. When I was young, I'd drawn the same number of pictures as cards in the Major Arcana, without the slightest conscious idea of what I was doing. I'd taken to calling them the Dog Arcana now.

I kept shuffling the cards on the table. I started feeling a small, pricking pain deep in my chest—as I always did.

The pain in my chest was just an illusion, but I was scared. Each time I told someone's fortune, I felt like... like I wanted to run away.

Like, what if the result was bad? What if I told them something bad, and messed up the futures of the people who wanted to know their fortunes?

It was easy to say that since I was just telling someone what their future would be like, I wasn't *really* responsible for what would happen. But from the perspective of the people I was talking to, that would just sound like an excuse. Right at this very moment, I was in a position where I could ruin somebody's future. That's why I was scared when I told fortunes.

But...

But I kept doing it. I had to.

I finished my shuffling and brought the cards back into a deck. Then I drew ten cards from the top and laid them facedown on the table. They were laid out in roughly the same shape as the Kabbalah—or Tree of Life—which connected the ten Sephirot.

I remembered a while ago, a professional tarot reader had gotten mad at me and told me I wasn't doing it quite right. From their perspective, it must have looked wrong.

But just as the Tree of Life was formed by the ten Sephirot, I put each card in its position.

All ten cards were facedown. Which ones I turned over depended on the nature of the request.

Since this request had to do with love, I should probably choose the Fourth Sephirah. I took a short breath, and then put my fingers on the card in the second row down on the right side of the Tree.

"Open, Chesed!"

Chesed was the Sephirah of kindness. It also symbolized holy love.

I didn't really have any reason for saying the name aloud. But

Chi had told me that it would be better to have some kind of cool catchphrase, so I did.

I looked at the screen and saw a huge flood of comments.

"There it is!"

"That catchphrase is so cool!"

"I'm in love!"

"She sounds like an otaku dork, lol."

"So cute!"

"Chesed-tan is my waifu."

"Do we get to see Myu's scary-ass pictures?"

"Her art's so bad it's good."

They were all a bunch of idiots. I decided to shake my head a little and forget all about them.

I concentrated and turned over the card. Before I could look at what the card said, a blurry vision flooded into my mind. It was kind of like the kaleidoscope effect you see on TV shows sometimes...

I saw two men in suits. Both were in their 20s. They were talking happily.

I saw spots in my field of vision as I came back to reality. I blinked a few times to figure out where I was. I'd been out for a maybe a little over a second. It had only taken an instant, but I'd seen it.

"Visions" was what I'd taken to calling them. It was a kind of spiritual power I'd had since I was very young. I didn't really know how they worked, but when I was listening to someone, I could somehow see fragments of their future.

Normally you called something like that clairvoyance, or maybe precognition, I think. But the vision I saw was a little strange, maybe. It didn't seem to match the question I'd been asked.

I looked at the card I'd turned over. It was a picture of a girl and an upside-down dog man. The girl was fused to the dog man's legs, and they were looking right at each other. The dog's body was covered in blood, and he looked like he'd collapsed, dead.

"The Hanged Dog. Reversed." This was the same card as the Hanged Man in a tarot deck. Reversed meant that from my perspective, it was upside-down.

"Hmm..." That explained it. I turned back to the camera and spoke to the listener.

"Mr. Mochi-Mochi Pon-Pon, can I ask you something? Is the person you're asking about maybe not a girl?"

"Huh?!" I heard a gasp on the other end of the phone.

The comment box was filled with confused questions.

Mr. Mochi-Mochi Pon-Pon had fallen silent. But I didn't want to ask any questions. It would feel like I was leading him if I did. So I waited patiently for him to talk.

And then...

"Wow. I guess I can't hide anything from you, can I, Myu? Yeah, that's right. The person I love is...a man."

I let out a gasp when I heard his courageous confession.

And I ignored the excited comments on the screen.

"Oh!"

"It's a homo."

"I'm a girl, and this made me wet."

"Didn't see that coming!"

"I'm gay...but he's not. He's straight. So I know if I ask him out, he'll hate me. But I can't keep hiding my love for him." The voice on the other side of the phone was mixed with sobs.

This had to be, like, so hard for him! So hard that he'd turned to an amateur fortune-telling stream like mine for help. It's okay, Mr. Mochi-Mochi Pon-Pon.

"There's no reason to give up. Really!"

"Huh?"

"I saw it in my vision. You and the guy you like were having, like, a super lovey-dovey conversation."

"Th-then..."

"You should tell him how you feel on a day that's important to you both! I think if you do, he'll understand!"

"R-really?! Thank you! You're my goddess, Myu! Thank you!" He thanked me excitedly, and hung up the phone.

Whew...I was glad that worked out. I was really glad I hadn't seen a bad future for him. Sometimes, even when I saw a good future for someone, I didn't have the emotional energy left to feel happy for them. This time, I could feel relieved. But it was always kind of a struggle for me.

I realized my hands were shaking. This happened every time I told somebody their fortune. I tried to hide my shaking hands by quickly bringing all the scattered cards back together. Then I glanced at the screen and saw it was overflowing with comments.

"Holy shit!"

"She got it!"

"Myu is our goddess! All hail Myu!"

"She's the real thing!"

"Myu's still got more tricks up her sleeve!"

"Lick-lick!"

"Stop with the licking, guys." It was creepy. But kind of funny, I guess.

"All right, time for our next little lost puppy to call in!" The phone started ringing before the words were even out of my mouth.

The second caller was a woman. She was calling to ask about a ring that she'd lost a month or so ago.

Just like with the first one, I used my cards to tell her fortune. In the vision I saw, a woman, who was probably the caller, was looking in the trunk of her car.

I told her the basic make and color of the car. I don't know a lot about cars, so I wasn't able to identify the model. But it matched the car that she owned exactly.

When I told her she'd dropped it in her trunk, she quickly went to look. Within three minutes, she was back, and excitedly told me that she'd found her ring.

Of all the things that people lost, stuff like rings were the easiest to find. Precious metals were especially good at storing people's feelings, the way a computer's hard drive stored data.

Then it was on to the third lost puppy. The man who answered the phone had a very androgynous voice.

"Hello, Myu? It's me! Zenigata! That's just my online name, though. Wow, I'm so happy I get to talk to you! I can't believe it! It's like I used up all my luck just for today! *Tee hee hee!* ☆ "

Wow. He was really excited and way too friendly. He almost sounded like a little kid.

I tried to think about if I had run into him before, but I couldn't come up with anything.

"So your name's Zenigata?"

"Yes, that's right. More specifically, it's 'Hello there, I'm Zenigata.'

I love Inspector Zenigata, you see."

"Huh? Inspector Zenigata? I'm sorry, I don't know who that is."

"Wow, teenage girls these days don't know about him?! Talk about a generation gap!"

"I-it's okay, sir!"

"No, you don't have to call me 'sir'! I'm still only 26!"

Wow, this was kind of a pain in the butt.

"By the way, I admire you almost as much as I admire Inspector Zenigata. I love the whole teenage girl fortune-teller thing. Oh, right. I have a question. Can you tell me what your hobbies are?"

"Wait, you can't just start asking me questions. For somebody who's 26, you sure sound like an old man."

All the listeners were saying things like, "Hang up on this asshole," "No one cares about you, loser," and, "Don't waste your time with this dipshit, Myu."

"Oh, I've got more than one question, though. I want to know what type of guys you're into. Try not to give me any obvious answers like, 'I'm into guys who are nice.' Oh, and do you ever think of becoming an idol? If you do, I'll back you all the way. I've got a government job, so I make some decent cash. Oh, am I not supposed to say that because it'll upset the peasants?"

"If you're not going to ask me to tell your fortune, I'm hanging up." My voice was cold, but when I saw Chi's whiteboard with "Calm down!" written in cute little letters, I almost laughed. *Thank you, Chi.*

"Oh, don't hang up! Don't hang up on me, please! I'm a huge fan!" Mr. Zenigata was panicking on the other side of the phone.

"So, Mr. Zenigata, what's your question for me?"

"Right, that's right! So, can I have you tell the future about anything?"

"*Hmm...* Maybe." My visions let me see just about anything. I couldn't choose whether what I saw was good or bad news for the questioner, though.

"Okay, here's my question."

I almost told him that he was supposed to be asking me for help, not peppering me with questions...but I figured it would just drag this out longer.

"Do you know the story about the man who livestreamed his game of One-Man Hide and Seek?"

It was something people had been talking about online. I'd heard a little about it from a classmate of mine who loved gossip.

Maybe it was just my imagination, but it felt like Mr. Zenigata's voice had changed. Like...I don't know. Like he'd suddenly gotten serious.

"I'd like you to use your fortune-telling to find out where the missing man is. Where he is, and whether or not he's alive."

I could see confused comments from the listeners. Most of the little lost puppies on my show so far had been asking me for help with things like romance or lost objects. Sometimes they'd just want to know what kind of luck they could expect to have in the future.

But it felt like this Zenigata guy was different. Of all the things he could ask, he wanted my help finding a famous missing person?

I think there was a similar show on TV once. Something where a self-proclaimed spiritualist would use their power to find missing people. They say all that stuff's fake, though.

I never thought somebody would ask me to do something like that.

"Myu, what's wrong? Can you not do it?"

Actually, maybe I could. Not that I really wanted to...

But if I did try to use my fortune-telling, I was scared I might see a bad vision. The pain deep in my chest flared up again.

But most of the listeners were telling me that I should do it.

I took a quick, inconspicuous glance over at Chi. She was watching me with an uneasy look on her face. Evidently, she didn't feel like she should be giving me instructions on her whiteboard.

What should I do?

I clenched my hands into fists. They were on top of my knees and out of the camera's view. Then I glared straight into the laptop's camera lens.

Miyuu, your power isn't wrong. It's okay to be proud of it.

"I'll try it." I made my decision and picked up the cards.

I was scared. I was seriously scared, but I had to be proud. That's what I had promised Dad.

Just like I'd done before, I laid out my hand-drawn cards in the shape of the Tree of Life. The one I needed to open this time was...

"Open, Yesod!"

The Ninth Sephirah. Its name meant "foundation."

Just as I turned over the third card in the center row, a vision came smashing into my brain...

The water's surface gently rocked. I was looking up at it. Was the sky so bright because it was a full moon outside? But my vision was blurry. It was like I was underwater, looking up. The moon's light couldn't reach down to the bottom of the water. I could barely make out the many shadows that wavered beside me.

"The bottom of the water. It's dark. They're not alone..." I described

what I was seeing without even realizing I'd opened my mouth. I'd
never seen anything like this before.

The room was deep in the back of a long, long hallway in a sub-basement, a place where even people with the right clearance rarely went.

It lacked the disinfectant smell unique to hospitals only because the place was almost entirely isolated from the outside. The bare concrete walls would have felt appropriate in a fallout shelter.

There was not a single window or a single ray of sunlight. The only light was a pale blue and came from the tablets held by several men who were sitting in a half-circle in the center of the room.

In the dim half-light, it seemed as if the room itself might continue off into endless darkness. Perhaps there was no furniture or other decoration in this room to help create this very illusion.

"A prophecy in the Old Testament tells us that in the end of days, the people will be branded with the mark of the Devil, '666,' and without that brand, they will be unable to survive." Standing opposite from the men in the circle was a man in a dark crimson suit, who began to speak in a loud, haughty tone.

All of the men in the circle were older than he was. But the man showed no signs of attempting to hide his arrogant attitude as he continued speaking. That meant he was the one in charge of this meeting.

"Of course, this is just a myth. But in reality, from the moment a human is born, you could say they're destined to be either one of the rulers or one of the ruled." One of the men, Hatoyama, a member of the Diet's lower house and a former prime minister, interrupted him.

"That's quite the statement, Mr. Takasu." There was a wry smile on his face. "Have we become some sort of dark religious cult or perhaps a shady secret society?"

"I take offense to that." The man in the crimson suit—Takasu—turned toward Hatoyama. He didn't appear to be terribly upset. "I am neither drunk on my own words, nor am I pretending to be part of the Illuminati."

"But isn't Mr. Hatoyama correct, in that now's not the time to be discussing legends and myths?" The next man to speak was a serious-looking sort in a while lab coat. Underneath the coat, he wore a shirt and necktie.

"Professor Matoba, I'm afraid the subject of my discussion is reality. I've taken this opportunity to make our position clear to everyone." Takasu looked around at the other men sitting in the half-circle, as if seeking agreement. "Our position as the rulers, you see."

A single image suddenly appeared on all the men's tablets. It consisted of several photographs of birds and dolphins.

But the animals weren't in their natural habitats. They were locked in outdoor pools or huge cages, being managed and controlled by human hands.

"These birds and dolphins have been implanted with microchips that allow them to be controlled remotely. We're already past the prototype stage. By applying a simple electrical signal to the parts of the brain that control neurotransmission, we can make them feel pain, joy, anger, or sorrow in a very natural manner. You're already aware of this technology, of course."

The sitting men nodded silently.

"Being controlled without realizing it is not necessarily a sad fate. And of course, it's not always wrong to control someone. It's possible for the rulers to give great happiness and satisfaction to the ruled. A look through the history books will show you that order has been destroyed by a handful of rioters several times. Humans are fundamentally stupid creatures, and without proper rule, their society will collapse from the inside. Strictly speaking, we're on a slow path to destruction right now. A haphazard response to this threat is meaningless, and thus, order must be brought about by a power that goes beyond normal conceptions of such. Thus—" Takasu paused, dramatically.

"What this world needs isn't a hero. It's a god."

The men seated in the half-circle began to whisper at the mention of such a fanciful being in a place like this. Takasu curled up his lips into a smile, as if enjoying their reaction.

PARANORMAL SCIENCE NVL

Occultic;Nine
オカルティック・ナイン

THERE IS NO SUCH THING AS THE "OCCULT." IT CAN ALL BE DISPROVED BY SCIENCE.
ONLY THOSE WHO HAVE ACCEPTED EVERYTHING
HAVE THE RIGHT TO KNOW THE TRUTH.

"You ever seen this before?"

I took out an envelope and showed it to the boy seated across from me. While the boy looked inside the envelope, I quickly glanced around the shop through my sunglasses.

I was inside a place called Amenity Dream, a trading card shop on Kichijoji's Sun Road. The shop was a little cramped, with several glass showcases displaying all kinds of cards in carefully organized rows.

There were five customers in the store right now, including me. Probably fewer than usual for this time of day. All of them were kids, either in middle school or elementary school. They all seemed to know one another, and were chatting with each other in loud voices. Sometimes, one of them would even shout or scream for some reason.

The young boy, who said his name was Sagami, and I were seated away from the others. There was a gaming area that seated up to thirty, and normally you'd see at least a couple groups of people playing. Fortunately for me, it was empty today.

Young Sagami's eyes went wide when he saw what was in the

envelope.

"Th-this is..."

"Don't tell anyone. If you do, you'll find yourself floating in Tokyo Bay," I warned him in a low whisper.

The other three were pretending to look at a showcase while shooting occasional glances our way. They seemed to be quite interested in our discussion.

"How did you get this?"

"I'll just say that in this world, money talks." I chuckled a little, and young Sagami began to grit his teeth.

"You grown-ups are all a bunch of cheaters, aren't you?"

"Heh. Say what you like."

"You'll really give this to me?"

"In exchange for information."

I took a new photo out from my coat pocket. It was a screenshot I'd taken of an internet video, showing a bespectacled man in his 20s who was looking at the camera.

"You ever seen him before?"

"Who is he?"

"A few days ago, a man doing a One-Man Hide and Seek livestream disappeared during the middle of it. This is that man."

"Oh yeah. The one from the article on Kirikiri Basara?"

"Oh, you read Kirikiri Basara?"

Kirikiri Basara, or KiriBasa for short, was an aggregator site for occult news stories. The site was popular among certain devoted fans of the genre.

I leaned in toward young Sagami. "That makes this quick, then. Strangely enough, the media isn't covering this matter at all. The only people online who are talking about it are at KiriBasa. This means someone's putting pressure on someone else. My guess is that the missing man has acquired some form of top-secret information."

"He didn't die from a curse because he was playing One-Man Hide and Seek?"

"No, he's not dead."

"How do you know?"

"How do I know, you ask?" I shrugged my shoulders in an exaggerated manner. "Because..."

I stood up and yanked off my sunglasses. "Because Myu said so!"

After hearing the name of my Ultra-Super Information Source, the whole shop went silent for several seconds. Everyone, not just young Sagami, was looking at me in surprise.

"Who's that? One of the new *Vanguard* characters?" he asked.

"It is not! I mean, sure, I think *Vanguard* definitely needs more female characters. But Myu isn't from the *Vanguard* anime. There's nothing in that little brain of yours but *Vanguard*, is there? You're going to be in your last year of middle school next year, right? Will be you be able to handle your exams?"

"Then who is it?"

"Wait, you're telling me you really don't know who Myu is?" I was so shocked that I had no choice but to pound my fists on the table. "You didn't see her Niconico stream yesterday?! How? Who? Get with the times, kid! The whole internet's starting to talk about this new teenage fortune-teller! She's going to go big for sure! How the hell can you not know who she is?! That's pathetic! Well, anyway,

Myu answered my question! She said the missing man is still alive! I'm the only person smart enough to ask her a question like that, you see! Well, it's like, when you've been watching her stream from the very beginning like I have, you can tell what sort of questions she wants you to ask. But anyway, she's incredibly accurate! She's the real deal! And since she said so, it *has* to be true! That's an absolute law! So the man isn't dead! He's still alive!"

"M-Morizuka, can you not pick fights with the little kids in my store?" the timid-looking owner said.

Oh, damn. I accidentally got serious at a middle school kid! The other customers were looking at me in shock. I tried my best to laugh it off. I bowed to the owner once, too.

"Sorry about that. Sagami here just said something so stupid, I was genuinely surprised. Tee hee! ☆" And then I stuck my tongue out, so I could be cute in an anime sort of way.

Neither the owner nor young Sagami laughed.

"But I will say this, though. My name isn't Morizuka. It's Moritsuka. Shun Moritsuka! Get it right already."

"Oh, sorry. Just try and keep it down." He didn't need to tell me. I wouldn't make the same mistake again.

I'm twenty-six years old, and a detective with the Musashino police, after all. I'm not just some kid.

"So can I have this card from Revenger, Raging Form Dragon, then?" Young Sagami waved the envelope I'd given him containing an extremely rare card for the *Vanguard* collectible card game.

"Huh?! What are you talking about, Sagami? I told you. It's in exchange for information. You didn't know anything about my question, did you? So you can't have it. Come on, give it back. Do you know how much I spent to get that thing?"

Between you and me, it was 5,000 yen. I paid 5,000 yen for a single card. And I had to go through a dozen trading card shops all over Tokyo to find it. No way in hell was I giving it to some middle school brat for nothing.

"Morizuka, you suck," young Sagami whined, despite the fact that I was his elder.

"Come on! How many times do I have to tell you? Are you sure you're in middle school? It's Moritsuka, not Morizuka! Now give me back my card!" I yanked it out of his hand.

Young Sagami pursed his lips into a pout. I wanted to do the same thing!

"Sagami, you shouldn't get so cocky just because you beat me in our last eleven *Vanguard* duels. Once you're done with middle school, you're not allowed to be proud of your *Vanguard* skills anymore."

"Aw, come on. Give it to me, Morizuka."

"No. And if you try to take it, that's larceny. Keep that in mind. If you don't, I'll arrest you on the spot. You don't want that, do you?" I waved the "Revenger, Raging Form Dragon" card in front of his face.

He was clearly getting mad. "I'm just a minor. They won't charge me."

"Wow, you think you're so smart, huh? Grown-ups hate kids like that, Sagami. You should cut it out." But he appeared to have no intention of listening to my warning.

"So, Morizuka, are we having a duel today?"

"Nope. I'm on the clock. Man, must be nice to be in middle school! Every day is like Sunday, isn't it? I'm so jealous. I wish I could do nothing but play *Vanguard* all day on a weekday."

"You're such a slacker. So what are you doing here?"

"Questioning people. That's my job. I just asked you for information, didn't I? Though I was wrong to try asking a kid whose only talent in life is *Vanguard*. Not that I expected much, of course. This is all just a game. A little game, like playing house. You understand now, don't you, Sagami? How hard it is to be a detective?"

"So you *are* slacking."

"I am not!"

This kid didn't know when to shut up. Even a nice guy like me was going to run out of patience eventually.

"So was the guy who was playing One-Man Hide and Seek a customer of ours or something?" The owner asked, confused.

I shrugged. "I don't know."

"You don't know?"

"But you know, the man I respect more than anyone, Inspector Zenigata, once said this." I closed my eyes and thought of the famous ICPO detective, who spent his life tracking down history's greatest thief. "'Even if you die 100 times, that's not the point. As long as a Lupin exists, I'm obliged to pursue him.' Well? Cool, huh? What a detective!"

"I don't know what that means..."

Just then, the famous *Lupin the 3rd* theme song started to play from my phone.

"Oh, sorry. This ringtone means it's an emergency. Might be a case!" I cut them off and quickly answered the phone.

"Agent Moritsuka?"

"Yeah."

The voice on the other send of the phone sounded further away than usual. I listened carefully. "Yeah... Yeah... Okay." When I finished, I hung up and sighed softly.

Young Sagami was looking at me in shock. "Hey, Morizuka, was the person on the phone talking to you in English?"

"Huh? Ahaha, you could tell, huh? Don't tell anybody else, okay? Anyway, I've gotta get back to work. Adieu!" I smiled and waved, then left the shop.

Amenity Dream was on the third floor of a multipurpose building. From the landing, you could look down and see people going up and down Sun Road.

"Now, then...looks like things are more serious than I thought. I need to get the thing from that anonymous tip before something really bad happens." I took the photo I'd shown to young Sagami out of my pocket and stared at the man's face.

"I guess this gets put off for a while." I pulled my fedora down low over my head and walked down the stairs. "'The bottom of the dark water,' huh? I guess my next stop is Tora no Ana in Shinjuku."

My vision was fading in and out. I was lying facedown on the counter at Café☆Blue Moon, and trying my best not to throw up.

In front of me was a glass half-filled with liquid. That was the cause of it all.

"Hey, hey! Gamota! There's no need to be so dramatic, is there?! Ryotasu said she liked it, you know?"

"Ryotasu's sense of taste is broken."

"It's yummy! ☆" Ryotasu was grinning. How could she possibly enjoy this awful concoction?

Master Izumin had just asked Ryotasu and me to try a new drink he'd come up with. I should've turned him down, but I let my curiosity get the better of me. Now, I was regretting it.

"What's in this stuff, anyway?"

"Oh, you didn't hear what I told Ryotasu? This is called Super Ultra Lucky Tea!"

What the heck?

"There's this magazine called *Kyam-Kyam* I always read..."

"Huh? Isn't that a fashion magazine for girls? You read that, Master Izumin?" I tried to imagine him grinning as he read the latest issue of *Kyam-Kyam*. It was frightening.

Not just frightening. Terrifying. The thought made my nausea worse.

"Jeez, Gamota, what's that supposed to mean? ♪ Why don't we go someplace dark and secluded so you can tell me all about it? ☆" Master Izumin posed like an innocent young maiden and winked at me. I managed to ignore him completely.

"Master, I'll take some water."

"That's so mean! How can you say that? I'm hurt!" He squirmed and contorted while he poured me a glass of water.

After I gulped down the ice-cold water, I started to feel a lot better.

"So anyway, *Kyam-Kyam*'s got this fortune-telling page in it that's supposed to be really accurate! It's so popular that it sells out the day the magazine's released! I've been buying that magazine forever, though, so if you ask me, it's just a huge nuisance. Anyway, the important thing is that it's got this fortune-telling page in it!"

"Don't tell me you gave me a lucky drink some fortune-teller told you to buy. That's just paid advertising! You fell for it! Wrong-sider! Fail!"

"Yeah! That's the thing!" He spun the ice tongs he was holding around as he nodded. "Just imagine how much of Japan's economy is based on fortune-telling these days!"

"Wh-what do you mean?"

"Every morning, all the TV channels do fortune-telling segments just before everybody is about to leave for work, school, or shopping, right? Some programs even do a little fortune-telling segment right after the weather."

That was true. I would watch those things before I left for school, too.

"Magazines are no different. The weekly magazines, the manga magazines, the fashion magazines; they've all got fortune-telling pages. And every day, newspapers and internet sites will tell you what your fortune is. Fortune-telling has unconsciously become a part of our daily lives! Not everybody believes them, but most people at least pay attention to what they say, don't they? When you're supposed to have good luck, you work extra hard that day. On days when you're supposed to have bad luck, you're more careful. If there happens to be a sale on your lucky item, you might buy it. Even if only 10% of Japan's population is being affected, even just a little, that's still over ten million people!"

Ten million people. That's a pretty big number, I thought.

"In other words, the Japanese as a race love fortune-telling more than you'd think! I love it, too! And since I'm a total slut, I'll read everything from Buddhist fortune-telling, to horoscopes, to feng shui!"

"Well, Japanese people always love to keep up with whatever the latest trend is. Not me, though."

"And so what I came up with was the Super Ultra Lucky Tea that you just tried. Every month, you've got a different lucky item, or lucky color, or lucky fruit, or lucky direction, et cetera. If I offer a drink that's got all that stuff in it, I'm sure it'll sell like bonkers! Ten million people will swarm my store! Oh no, what should I do, Gamota?"

No, that's not happening. And where did you get that 10% number to begin with, anyway? Also, that wasn't what I asked. I asked what was in this awful drink.

He'd told me that I could sit in the shop in the evenings when it wasn't busy in exchange for testing out his new drink menu, and I'd been only too happy to oblige. But the thought of drinking more of these things in the future made me feel really depressed.

"You've got such feminine tastes for a guy with a face like yours, Master Izumin. I don't believe in fortune-telling at all. It's no different than the occult. Oh, maybe I'll do some fortune-telling stuff on Kirikiri Basara! And then the Basariters can just rip it apart. There's probably a lot of people who think like I do—"

"Ga~ Mo~ Ta~ N! ☆"

"Awhooahh!"

Ryotasu's finger was tracing a line down my back. It was so ticklish, I couldn't help but shake.

"Gamotan, you don't believe in fortune-telling? But you said that girl's fortune-telling was 'just right,' didn't you?"

"Huh? That girl?"

Ryotasu's eyes were looking past me at the small TV on the other side of the counter. There was a girl on the screen that I remembered. I'd seen her just a few days ago, and there was no way I could forget her.

"Wait, that's Myu!"

She was sitting on a park bench, looking slightly embarrassed as she answered questions from a female reporter.

"Master! The sound! Turn up the volume!"

"Oh, you know her, Gamota? Is she your girlfriend?" I ignored his sarcasm and focused on the screen.

The text on the screen said, "The Big Thing Online! Super-Popular

High School Fortune-Telling Girl, Myu Aikawa." This TV was a real TV, not a computer monitor. So it was probably one of the evening news variety shows that was on...*Don't Miss It! POM!*, I think.

So she was on TV, which meant—

"Myu's making her TV debut on *Don't-POM*? Let's call her Myu-Pom! This is going to be big."

"Hey, that's Inokashira Park, isn't it?"

Come to think of it, I recognized the area, too. That was the park, all right.

"Does she live near Kichijoji?"

"Want to go see her? I'll go with you! ☆"

"Nah, this isn't a live broadcast."

I stared at Myu-Pom's face as I spoke. This terrestrial digital broadcast had much better quality than the Niconico videos I'd seen before. I could see her face clearly. I could even see her pores. I could stare right into Myu-Pom's pores.

"Yeah, just right! Even on TV, she's just right!"

"Just right! ♪ Just-just-just-right!" Ryotasu suddenly started to sing and dance again, but I ignored her.

"'Just right' is the perfect way to describe Myu-Pom's looks, you know? You know, she's like the third-cutest girl in a class. The fact that she's not some amazing beauty actually makes her more approachable. Well, since she's not an idol or anything to begin with, that lack of refinement may just add to her charms. Her breasts are like what, a C cup? D cup? Yeah, just right. Not too big and not too small. She's not too serious. She talks like a teenage girl but she doesn't look like a skank. She's just the right degree of approachable. Like if you asked her, she'd probably give you some chocolate on Valentine's Day even if she didn't really mean anything by it. That's the feeling I get."

Yeah. Just right.

Just right.

Juuust right.

Very, *very* just right.

"Gosh, I can tell Gamota's never had sex even once before. I don't know why you'd think anyone would be interested in your opinion. Oh, but it's still so cute! ♪ " Ryotasu chirped.

You telling me I'm cute just makes me shiver. Not that I would actually say that out loud.

"Well, if I had to point out one thing about her that wasn't perfect, it would be that moe anime voice thing she's doing. It feels a little fake. Also, maybe if she could just change the way she talks a little. The rest is fine!"

The program on TV kept Myu-Pom's real name, school, and anything else that could identify her a secret. They seemed to just be introducing her as a popular internet fortune-teller. Myu-Pom was a little nervous, but she was smiling as she answered the reporter's questions. Gradually, she was starting to relax.

But the last time I'd watched her stream, a mean caller had trolled her so hard she'd broken down and cried. Since seeing a girl my age break down and cry was a new experience for a guy like me, I couldn't take my eyes off it. That guy was such an asshole. How could you make Myu-Pom cry?

But the way she'd hidden her crying face with her hood while her shoulders shook had been just utterly amazing. It had instantly turned me into a Myu-Pom fan. The guys on 2ch had loved it, too.

When was this interview recorded? Was it before that? Or after?

"When I'm listening to someone's voice, I get a glimpse of their future. I call these glimpses 'visions.' And then I use those visions to give them, like, basic advice?" I sighed a little when I heard what Myu-Pom said.

When I watched "Myu's Niconico Live Fortune-Telling" last time, she'd talked about a bunch of visions she'd seen. One of them gave me a sense of déjà vu. It was when she was talking to the third caller.

This is what she'd said:

The bottom of the water. It's dark. They're not alone...

The man's in the water. He's surrounded by other people. There's a full moon in the sky...

I'd actually had a similar dream a month before. It happened when I fell asleep in class once. The dream felt like it had run on for a long, long time. When I woke up, I was worried I'd been asleep for hours, but it had actually only been a few seconds.

The unsettling gap between reality and the way it had felt was so great that I remembered it very clearly. The dream had been just like the vision that Myu-Pom had described.

In the dream, I was lying at the bottom of the water, surrounded by many people, and staring up at a brilliant full moon that shone down from above the water's surface. I particularly remembered the coldness of the water. When I woke up, I'd actually shivered. Had Myu-Pom seen the same thing?

"That's possible... No—actually, it's not."

Talk about synchronicity. There was no way that could be true. If I really did have the same dream as Myu-Pom, that would be something like fate. But this wasn't a manga or an anime, so that was impossible.

"*Hmm...* Myu Aikawa. I've heard that name somewhere." Master

Izumin had stopped getting the bar ready and was watching TV with me. Suddenly, he tilted his head and spoke.

"A relative, maybe? Or is she your daughter?" I thought that meant that maybe, if I came to this café a lot, I could meet her. But then I realized that if I did, it would be all I could do to even talk to her. That was kind of depressing.

It was hard to imagine a girl like Myu-Pom being the daughter of a pervert like this. That was even more impossible than the two of us having the same dream.

The program kept going on as I sat there thinking. The stupid-looking reporter was explaining Myu-Pom to the audience as if she was really impressed.

"Not only is she online, she's also got a fortune-telling segment in a magazine! And they say it's really accurate!"

"Oh, right! This is it!" Master took out the issue of *Kyam-Kyam* he'd showed me earlier, as if he'd just remembered something. He scanned the fortune-telling page he loved and finally pointed to some tiny letters in the corner.

"Take a look!"

The letters said:

"Advisor: Myu Aikawa."

"Oh wow! She's in here, too!"

Maybe she did a lot of work as a fortune-teller. But from the stream I'd seen, it didn't feel like she was charging for her services like professional fortune-tellers did.

"She's always been really good to me. I think she's a lot more amazing than your average idol, you know?"

The program ended with Myu-Pom telling the reporter's romantic future. The narrator said, "We can't wait to see what she does next!" And then Myu-Pom disappeared into Kichijoji Station.

First Inokashira Park, and now this. Why were they pushing Kichijoji so hard? Maybe she lived near here? Then maybe I'd run into her in front of the station! Wow, wouldn't that be awesome?!

I wish I knew what high school she went to. She hadn't been wearing her uniform during the interview, so there was no easy way to tell.

It was just a five-minute segment, but it was still amazing to think that they'd give that much time to an amateur Niconico streamer. When I looked on Twitter—

"It's trending at #1!" This was gonna be big. In a good way.

It was safe to say I was witnessing the birth of a new idol. This was exciting.

"That's right! Kirikiri Basara's gotta get in on this big wave, too!"

Myu Aikawa was a teenage fortune-teller. Like I'd just said, fortune-telling was absolutely an occult topic. In other words, it was safe to put her on Kirikiri Basra.

"Time to find some screencaps of today's program!" I checked the comment board on 2ch.

Nobody had uploaded the video yet, but there were plenty of pictures of the segment. *Thanks for pulling my screencaps for me, 2ch-ers.* Taking text from 2ch was against the rules, but copying and pasting an image fell into a gray area.

All I had to do was put up a breaking news update with a shorter comment than usual. What was important now was speed.

**[Breaking News] "Teenage Fortune-Teller Myu Makes Her TV Debut!"
[So Cute]**

■**NEET God**

So she was on TV, which meant—

Q

T

3.14! ♪

Also, I wasn't that interested in her fortune-telling. So, you guys gonna rip her apart? Are you willing to rip apart a high school girl? Even if she's so cute?

Though part of me wants to see Myu-Pom crying after you're done with her lol

"Okay, and that's upped!" *Excellent work, if I do say so myself.*

This could be my chance to rack up a huge number of views. All that was left was to watch and enjoy Ryotasu's weird dance, and see what my Basariters would do.

"Ryotasu, do a dance for me."

"Poyaya? Just one? I could do a hundred!"

"Do your favorite, then."

"*Hmm...* I'll pass. Get lost, loser! ☆"

"Hey!"

She was always willing to dance when nobody wanted her to, but she wouldn't take requests?

"A woman's heart is like an autumn sky. It's hard to say what it will be like at any given moment." I didn't like the way Master Izumin was grinning.

But an hour or so later, I'd forgotten all about that.

"Whoa! Look at the hit counter!" *Should we call this the Myu-*

Pom Effect? My breaking news article on Myu-Pom was getting hits at a pace I'd never seen before. And given the nature of my site's commenters, most of the posts were pretty friendly to her.

1. Anonymous Tells It Like It Is
| I don't buy that shit for a second lol

2. Anonymous Tells It Like It Is
| omg kyoot

3. Anonymous Tells It Like It Is
| I bet she's paying for this article, too. But yeah, she's cute.

4. Anonymous Tells It Like It Is
| Tell my fortune, baby! lolol

5. Anonymous Tells It Like It Is
| Change

6. Anonymous Tells It Like It Is
| Another shady fortune-teller? Japanese people sure do love them.

7. Anonymous Tells It Like It Is
| But is she cute? I like her voice. It sounds like Yukarin's.

8. Anonymous Tells It Like It Is
| She's just a little shy of being center stage in a 48.

9. Anonymous Tells It Like It Is
| Myu is the dumbest fucking name. Where can I go to meet her?

10. Anonymous Tells It Like It Is
> She can tell MY fortune, IYKWIMAITYD.

11. Anonymous Tells It Like It Is
> Literally who is this ugly bitch?

12. Anonymous Tells It Like It Is
> Only stupid wrong-sider skanks would believe this bitch. I want to
> lick her tits.

13. Anonymous Tells It Like It Is
> Myu! I love you!

14. Anonymous Tells It Like It Is
> I've followed her fortune-telling stream since the first episode.
> Myu is such a sweet girl. She's very polite for a teenage girl these
> days. I want to marry her.

I guess everyone fell in love with Myu's just-right beauty. I understood. I knew exactly how they felt.

If she'd been a little less cute, they probably would've been brutal to her. She was very close to the line.

"Oh, even Sarai's commenting." Sarai had never commented this soon after an article went up. I couldn't imagine a guy like him falling in love with Myu-Pom, though.

Fortune-tellers are all frauds. They're no different than con men. Whether it's some random girl with a reputation for always being right, or a celebrity fortune-teller on TV, or a fortune-teller in a magazine, they're all the same.

They're all just using reading techniques. They do research on the target, in one form or another, before the actual fortune-telling takes place. Then, when it's time, they act like they have real psychic powers. The ignorant target just sits there in awe as the "fortune-teller" gets one thing after another right. So the power of suggestion takes over. After that, they'll believe any half-assed piece of advice they're given. That's the method fortune-tellers on TV use. It's called hot reading.

Of course, a fortune-teller who's got a shop and has to work with anybody who walks in the door can't use that technique. So what do they do? They use something called cold reading. They make it look like they're just making small talk, but they'll actually lead the conversation in directions that tell them what they want to know about their target. Myu Aikawa isn't using cold reading, though. While it's fraudulent, it also takes some serious ad-libbing skills, so it's probably too hard for her.

Either way, there's probably some agency behind her that's trying to set her up as a celebrity or idol. This is all a farce they've set up. She'll probably make her celebrity debut soon. This TV segment was definitely planned in advance. It's just viral marketing.

Man, why so serious? I wanted to ask.

His comments were exactly the same as ever. For a Basariter, that gave him a perfect score. But since everybody else was talking about how cute Myu-Pom was, he was the odd man out. The other Basariters were dogpiling him.

217. Anonymous Tells It Like It Is

If you're that sure she's a fraud, then you call her. Then you'll get rekt.

218. Anonymous Tells It Like It Is

A battle between Sarai and Myu-Pom, huh? Reminds me of that "scientist versus psychic" thing they did about 20 years ago. I loved that.

219. Anonymous Tells It Like It Is

Forget that. Guys, I want to make Myu my little sister. How do I do that? Also, admin, stop calling her Myu-Pom, you freak.

220. Anonymous Tells It Like It Is

If Sarai was able to prove she was cheating, Myu might cry! If you do that I'll never forgive you, Sarai!

221. Anonymous Tells It Like It Is

[Breaking News] "Sarai Says He'll Make a Teenage Girl Cry"

222. Anonymous Tells It Like It Is

Let's go to the sea, Brother. You love the sea, right?

223. Anonymous Tells It Like It Is

Sarai: "It's all the plasma's fault."
Yeah, that's it.
Go study with professor Dai*** you hardhead.

224. Anonymous Tells It Like It Is

Kirikiri Basara sends our own Sarai onto the field!
You guys ready to shoot him from behind?
Shoot the bastard!

225. SARAI

All right. If you're that insistent, then I'll do it. The next time Myu Aikawa streams, I'll call her.

226. Anonymous Tells It Like It Is

Woah...

227. Anonymous Tells It Like It Is

You think you're hot shit, don't you lol
You're obnoxious

228. Anonymous Tells It Like It Is

The next Niconico Live Fortune-Telling is tonight. If you do show up, I'll be cheering on Myu, 'kay?

229. Anonymous Tells It Like It Is

Several days later, we find Sarai, his ass thoroughly kicked by a teenage girl...

230. Anonymous Tells It Like It Is

Well, there's no telling if Sarai's call is even going to get through. Actually, the odds are pretty damn low lol

231. Anonymous Tells It Like It Is

You think Sarai-kyun might be worried that Myu's going to take his position at Kirikiri Basara? Don't worry man. Everyone here already hates you.

232. Anonymous Tells It Like It Is

Go get your ass owned, Sarai.

"Wow, Sarai doesn't know how to handle it when people are trying to provoke him. The best thing to do at a time like this is grin and be self-effacing, and try to suck up to them."

"Huh? But Gamota, weren't you arguing with all those egg people earlier? You were talking to yourself when you did."

"Ghhnn…"

Of course, that was a lot easier to say when you weren't the one on the receiving end. Even a saint would snap if he was the one one being trolled.

"But, Master Izumin, does that mean Sarai and I are on the same level? That arrogant, nerdy tryhard Sarai is on the same level as me, the NEET God? Aw, poor Sarai! I had no idea you were such a loser! We should go drinking together sometime!" Not that I'd ever been drinking.

"Hahaha, look at you get mad. You really *are* a kid, Gamota. ♪ " Master Izumin was grinning at me. It was so creepy, I felt a shiver run down my back.

"But I'm interested in seeing this Sarai kid go up against Myu Aikawa. As a reader of the *Kyam-Kyam* fortune-telling page, I'm on her side."

I was going to watch tonight's livestream no matter what. Could there be a better way to get some hits? I envisioned myself writing about it, getting a million hits, and getting rich off the affiliate income.

After Sarai's declaration that he would appear on Niconico Live Fortune-Telling, the comments on my article started speculating about who would be the winner. In just two hours after upload, the number of comments had already exceeded the total for articles like "Man Livestreams One-Man Hide and Seek, Never Comes Back," and

"The Curse of Kokkuri-san Is Seriously Terrifying."

"Ryotasu, the day I buy you some yogurt may not be that far off. How about we go right now?" But when I looked around the shop, Ryotasu was nowhere to be found.

"Ryotasu left already."

"She left?!"

That's so mean. How could she leave without saying anything? It made me really sad. Especially since I was going to go get yogurt with her.

"Can you go home too, Gamota? It's about time for the night's customers to arrive." It was only when he told me that I realized it was already dark outside.

"The NEET God shall, like a true NEET, leave by himself! I'm not crying!" I needed to get home and get ready for the stream, anyway.

"Oh, read this, Master." I passed him a sheet of paper.

"Huh? What's this? A love letter?"

"Hey, don't be creepy, please? It's my suggestions for how to improve that weird lucky tea stuff you made me drink."

"Huh, really? That's a big help. I don't really know what young boys are into, you see. ♪ That's so nice of you, Gamota. ♪ "

"I-It's not like I'm trying to thank you for letting me stay here all the time. I just don't want to drink any more of that nasty stuff, is all."

It's just to protect myself, I thought. *Next time, give me something better tasting, okay? Bye!*

I quickly ran out of the café.

Master Izumin said, in a sweeter tone than usual, "Come back soon!" But it was so creepy, I didn't even want to respond.

PARANORMAL SCIENCE NVL

Occultic;Nine

オカルティック・ナイン

THERE IS NO SUCH THING AS THE "OCCULT." IT CAN ALL BE DISPROVED BY SCIENCE.
ONLY THOSE WHO HAVE ACCEPTED EVERYTHING
HAVE THE RIGHT TO KNOW THE TRUTH.

▶ site 08: MMG

"Is there some reason you're bringing up RFID chips again?" Hatoyama seemed irritated as he spoke.

"That plan was a massive failure. I've never seen such a poorly thought-out plan."

"Some of the donors even claimed to suffer health problems. And the whole thing almost came to light," Matoba added with a frown.

"Um, what happened to that one man? What was his name? The traitor."

"Aaron Russo."

Hatoyama nodded when Takasu said the name. "Yes, him. Was he properly 'dealt with'?"

"Yes. There were no issues." Takasu said no more.

It would be inappropriate to go into the details in a place like this. All everyone needed to know was that the traitor had been dealt with.

"It was actually during the information suppression after he was dealt with where you were very helpful, Mr. Hatoyama."

Hatoyama chuckled and waved his hands in front of his face. "I don't mind. It's not my money. Japan's 'Freedom of the Press' ranking has dropped to 65. It's dropped even lower after the passage of the State Secrecy Law. Some of the younger Diet members say that this was something to be ashamed of, but it certainly does come in handy. Since everyone in the country thinks they're free, there's no room to doubt that it's peaceful."

"You have the whole public thinking you're a clown, Mr. Hatoyama. Very cunning of you."

Hatoyama smiled, pleased with Matoba's statement. "It makes things easier, you see. The matter with the 'occult' is proceeding apace as well, then?"

"Yes, of course." Takasu nodded respectfully. "The idea of turning the failed RFID project into an urban legend to bury it was quite bold."

Matoba shrugged. "The first time I heard it, I was terrified at what might happen."

"Either way, I'd prefer we stopped discussing the microchips. I don't want to hear about any of our Dark History. Can you tell me how the new plan is going? Don't tell me it's failed so hard, you're already praying to God for help?" He was smiling, but there was no laughter in his eyes.

In his eyes, Matoba and the others caught a glimpse of the cunning man who played the fool, and shivered.

But Takasu ignored him and gave a small shrug. "Dark History, huh? It's true that the RFIDs were a failure. But there's nothing to be learned from success. And there is much to be learned from the history of failure. It is critical that we not become arrogant. We are, after all, the rulers."

By the time I got back to the editing department, the sun had almost set.

"I'm back!" I said, but there were only two or three people there to hear me. They all glanced at me, waved and said hello, then went back to their work. The others were probably all still out working.

There was only a week until the next issue had to be ready, but the place felt lifeless. That was a common sight lately.

The twenty-four-story building I was in, just five minutes' walk from Gotanda Station, looked very nice from the outside. Since the company located there sold textbooks, academic books, and other serious works, it was probably important for them to maintain a proper exterior.

But there was a corner on the sixteenth floor that was very different than the others.

Mumuu Monthly. It was a monthly magazine that dealt with the occult. It had a lot of history, and it had gotten its start long before I'd been born. But these days, if someone was talking about it, you could expect them to be laughing.

Its editing department was blocked off from the rest of the floor with shelves, and there was stuff piled almost all the way up to the ceiling. For some reason, some of the lights were always turned off, which gave the whole place a gloomy look. According to the editor-in-chief, it was to save electricity, but I thought there was probably a much less high-minded reason for it. Compared to the rest of the building, the *Mumuu* editing department was a mess.

There were old, yellowed document drafts crammed haphazardly onto the shelves. What looked like ancient texts (but probably weren't) lay in piles on the floor. There was some kind of huge stone sculpture that reflected some garish color in the light, and a strange life-sized statue—the kind you'd find overseas—holding a spear. There was even a little torii altar behind one of the shelves. All that weird stuff made it incredibly hard to see.

The company had only moved into this building a few years ago. In that short time, we'd easily made much more of a mess than any of the other departments. No one ever talked about cleaning it up, though. Everyone seemed to prefer it this way.

Not me, though. Not really. Maybe it was just because my sixth sense was a lot stronger than your average person's. That torii altar and all that other stuff didn't make the place lucky. Quite the opposite, probably. And personally, I found it really creepy. Thanks to all that, when I went into the women's bathroom alone at night, I'd hear voices that weren't really there.

Thanks to my power, I'd had all kinds of awful experiences.

"Maybe it's fate that I'm working for an occult magazine," I muttered to myself.

Surprisingly, very few people in *Mumuu*'s editorial department had a strong sixth sense. Quite the opposite, in fact. And the things I told them were such common stories that they didn't even think they were worth writing about.

I weaved my way through shelves that threatened to collapse at any minute and headed for my desk in the back of the department. "I'm so tired... Maybe I should've had the veggie and extra garlic ramen at Ramen Saburo." I sighed and sat down.

I'd been in Kichijoji doing research on a story, so I'd thought about stopping, but for a magazine editor like me who was running around doing interviews every day of the week, anything with extra garlic was strictly forbidden. So I'd been forced to skip it. I used to go all the time when I was a student, but once I'd gotten a job, I'd almost entirely stopped.

I took off my heels and tossed them under my desk, then sighed. The shoulder where I'd been carrying my bag was stiff. I tried giving it a little massage, but it didn't help me.

My bag was stuffed full. It held my laptop, my drafts, my reference documents, and my notebook, all of which I needed for work, as well as a camera.

I took the camera out of my bag. I hadn't had a chance to use it today, either. Well, there weren't going to be many chances for an editor at an occult magazine to use a high-powered camera like this. It was really kind of a waste.

The camera was just a hobby of mine. It wasn't part of my job. Cameras these days were easy to use, and supposedly, even girls like me were getting into them. I'd gotten into it, figuring that it wouldn't hurt with my job.

I was getting a little sick of it now, though. It was just taking up space. The camera itself was very compact, but if you included the lens, it was bigger than you'd think. *Maybe I should just leave it at home,* I thought.

I rubbed my shoulder and looked at my desk, where I saw an envelope I didn't remember putting there. The handwriting on the front said "Isayuki Hashigami #26."

"Ascension!" Oops. I said my favorite word again. It was useable in almost any situation, so I had a habit of saying it all the time. I'd like to fix that, but it had proven impossible.

"Mr. Hashigami's latest article's ready, huh? I should've stopped by and gotten it. Did Makabe pick it up for me, maybe?" For the past two years or so, Isayuki Hashigami, a professor at Seimei University, had been writing a column for *Mumuu.* The next issue would mark his twenty-sixth column. Last spring, his old editor had transferred to another department, and I'd taken over for him.

Dr. Hashigami's house was in Kichijoji, too. But the article itself had a clear deadline, and he hadn't said anything to me, so I hadn't stopped by his house today.

I looked around the room for Makabe, but his desk was empty. Did he drop the draft off and leave again?

"Nah, knowing him he's probably off having a relaxing lunch somewhere. Not that it's lunchtime." The new employees had a tendency to slack off at times, I thought. Though to be fair, I'd only joined the company a year before Makabe.

I decided to read it immediately. "Let's see. 'Why We Should Be Less Emotional About Ghosts,' huh? Interesting."

Whether you believe in ghosts or not, you're probably too emotional about them... is what Dr. Hashigami had said. That emotion was clouding our eyes to the truth and stopping us from seeing the true nature of the phenomenon.

"—When you think of a ghost, what do you think of? Do you think of a person? If you do, you're already too emotionally involved."

"I see. So maybe believers are more prone to preconceptions than non-believers." Personally, I liked this new theory of Dr. Hashigami's.

After the Mayan prophecy in 2012 had failed to amount to anything, it had become the subject of vicious online mockery. A famous source of articles we'd been using since the turn of the century was gone. Lately, there'd only been smaller topics to write about, and I remembered hearing the head editor complaining about declining sales. But now, we had this new occult boom helping us out.

Dr. Hashigami had switched to believing in the occult, and his articles, discussing his attempts to research it from a scientific perspective, were gaining in popularity. It was like night and day compared to the first column he'd written for us. It felt like something must have happened to him, but...what could it have been?

"Hey, Sumikaze. You back?" I heard the voice of our head editor, Takafuji. He was the one who'd made such a mess out of the editing department. He was also a man who insisted on not dressing up, wearing a polo shirt and blazer at all times. If the hem of his polo shirt hadn't been tucked in to his pants, I might have been able to show him a little bit of respect, but that didn't seem to concern him in the slightest.

His skills as an editor, however, were worthy of respect. In the two years since he'd taken over the department, *Mumuu's* sales had almost doubled, supposedly. Given the fact that the Mayans were lost to us as a source of income, that was pretty incredible.

"Dr. Hashigami's article looks good this time."

"Did you read it already?" Usually, he wouldn't look at it this early.

"Hey, who do you think got it for you?"

"It was Makabe, right?"

"It was me! Me!"

"You did it yourself? *Hmm...* I hope that that's not a sign of something ominous. Are we going to get attacked by UFOs from the Large Magellanic Cloud tomorrow?"

"Nah. If we were, someone I know would've told me about it. I've got connections all over the world, you see."

"Ahaha! It was just a joke. You're too old to be proud of knowing people like that, aren't you?" Supposedly, it was true that he knew people all over the world, though. He'd been working at *Mumuu* since it was founded, after all.

"Anyway, I happened to have something else to take care of in Dr. Hashigami's neighborhood. I figured that while I was there, I should pick it up."

"I see. You're really spoiling Makabe, aren't you?"

"Don't be stupid. I sent him on an emergency day trip to Yamanashi instead."

"I take that back. That's a dick move."

"Haha."

One of the older editors told me that he used to have a much more severe personality. But lately, he'd relaxed enough that he'd even talk to new girls like me. Maybe it was just because sales were good. The same older editor had told me that before I joined, we didn't even have the money to send people on long-distance trips.

"Still, thanks for getting it for me." I stood up and bowed. "If only Dr. Hashigami would get a computer. Then we wouldn't have to go pick his stuff up, you know."

I loved his work, but going all the way to Dr. Hashigami's house every month was a bigger hassle than you'd think. I'd have been happier if he could have just sent it over email, but maybe people of his generation didn't like that.

Still...I didn't like that house. Well, there was something about it that my sixth sense didn't like.

"So, hey, Sumikaze. Is Dr. Hashigami kind of a misanthrope?"

"Huh? What do you mean?"

"When I went to get the draft, his mom answered the door. I asked if he was away, and she said he was home. I wondered if it might have been rude for me to just come barging over like that."

"I don't think so. Whenever I go pick up the drafts, he always talks to me. And...wait, his mom? Not his wife?"

"Yeah, she looked like she was in her seventies."

"Huh..." I'd been to his house over ten times, and I'd never met his mother.

"Wait, does he live with his mother?"

"I don't know the answer to that, I'm afraid."

I searched my memories, and quickly found an answer. "Oh, his mom died a long time ago, I think?" I pulled the folder that held all his drafts out from the desk.

It was my policy to always keep things neat and organized, so my desk was clean, even if the rest of the office wasn't. "He talked about how his mom was dead in an article last year." I flipped through the files, and sure enough, his eighteenth article talked about how his

mother was deceased.

"You're right. But, you know, it was definitely an old lady who answered the door."

Maybe a relative? But why couldn't he or his wife come to the door themselves? His college-aged son was there, too.

It seemed very strange to have that woman answer the door.

"There's an ascension for you. Do you think that she might have been..."

"Might have been...?"

I looked around the room and lowered my voice. "A ghost?"

The editor-in-chief furrowed his brow and thought for a second, before slapping his hands against his knees. "That's just great! I've been working for *Mumuu* for thirty years, and I can't even tell when an old woman's a ghost! I guess we've still got a lot to learn, huh?" He cackled and walked back to his desk, scratching his back with a ruler.

I wasn't joking, though. Maybe it was best just to drop it. I didn't have the right to inquire into his family matters, and as long as we had his article, that was all we needed.

A better editor might have made the choice to dig deeper. But I didn't want too many people finding out about my sixth sense. I'd learned over the twenty-three years of my life that it was better not to let people find out.

So I put it aside and went back to thinking about my own article.

I took my reporter's notebook out of my bag and opened it to the page of notes I'd taken today. I was looking at a case where an underage girl had spent a year living with a mummified man. Lately, people had even been talking about it on the internet. The editor-in-chief had thought there might be shamanistic or ritual elements involved, and told me to write an article about it.

The incident itself had been discovered about two years ago. The police had gotten involved, and news articles were written, though they were brief.

It happened at a big mansion on the outskirts of Kichijoji. That's where the tragedy had taken place. I'd actually gone to the vicinity of the mansion to do some research, and learned quite a few things. The head editor had been right that this was worth looking into. There were a lot of things that couldn't be easily explained.

The basic outline of the case involved an older brother who died due to medical malpractice. His younger sister, who was fifteen at the time, spent roughly a year living with his corpse. The mummy man and the girl were siblings. That was fine. It made sense.

What was strange was that the brother's body had already been given a death certificate by a doctor. So after that, who got it to the mansion, and how? No hospital or funeral home would do such a thing.

"If the mummy walked home on his own, that sounds pretty occult to me. Actually, he'd be closer to a zombie than a mummy then." I'd been hoping I could write my article on that aspect of the case, but I'd eventually come to the conclusion that it was impossible. I'd decided to head back to the office for the day.

This was just a criminal matter. It would be hard to find anything occult related to it. A girl living with a corpse was weak material for an article by itself. But that didn't mean I could tell the head editor that this was a bad idea. My pride as a journalist wouldn't let me.

The reason he hadn't asked me anything a moment ago was probably because he trusted me. That's why I wasn't ready to give up just yet. "Still, there's not too much I can do..."

I couldn't go and make something up. The head editor had been quite clear about that when I joined the department. But without some type of occult content, there wasn't any point in *Mumuu* writing about it. Personally, I was willing to write with another focus, but I couldn't just ignore the magazine's genre.

"I wonder if there's anything good online." I just needed something to give me a place to start. The mummy incident had been discovered two years ago, but suddenly people online were talking about it. They might know something I didn't.

I started by searching the name of the little sister—Seria Mina. When the police had announced the case, they'd left her name out of it, so it might not be on the internet yet.

"*Hmm...*" It was a rare name, so there weren't many hits. The only perfect match was a certain Facebook page.

There was only one person on it who used the name "Seria Mina." Was she the girl I was after? I'd just have to take a look and see.

I was surprised to find a lot more posts than I expected. She'd been keeping a diary online for over five years. It would take time to read it all.

"Maybe I should've stopped at Saburo after all..." I sighed and drooled a little. Then I popped a piece of milk candy that I kept at the side of my desk into my mouth to assuage my hunger. *Time to get to work.*

I decided I'd start by reading the posts from three years ago. As soon as I started reading, I saw something strange. All of the posts were about her older brother. You could call the thing a "big brother diary" if you wanted.

MARCH 20TH.
----

*Brother was nice enough to take me for a drive in his
car this afternoon. He knows I don't get out much, so
he even took time off work. But my brother just got his
license, so he's not very good at driving. He's not good
with directions, and got lost several times. In the end, we
didn't make it to Shonan Beach.*

*"I'm sorry. Next time I'll memorize the map," Brother said
as he slumped his shoulders.*

*You know, Brother, I'm very happy just to sit next to you.
Just driving with you for hours was enough to make me
want to cry. Perhaps God heard my wish that we never
make it to the beach, and did that for me as a favor. Take
me again, please, okay?*

She seemed to have some kind of weird thing for her older brother. Of course, maybe she couldn't help it. If this Seria Mina was the same as the one from the mummy case, her parents would have already been dead. She and her brother would have been using the vast fortune they inherited to survive. If he was the only family she had, that might explain her dependence on him.

It struck me as odd, though, that even though she would've been fourteen at the time, from reading her diary, I got the impression that, psychologically, she was much younger. I decided to throw away any preconceptions I had and proceed on the assumption that this Seria Mina was a different person.

MAY 12TH

Let's go to the sea, Brother. You love the sea, right?

MAY 13TH

Brother asked me to make his favorite dish, French toast, today. I'm quite clumsy, and I'm always reliant on my older brother. But making French toast is the one thing that I'm better than him at. Mother taught me how to do it herself, after all. It's the one thing I can do to make Brother happy. He was so happy when he ate it this morning. He even said he wanted to eat it every day for the rest of his life. Tee hee! Brother, that sounds like a marriage proposal. If I wasn't his little sister, I might have accepted. No, I prefer being Brother's little sister.

MAY 14TH

Let's go to the sea, Brother. You love the sea, right?

MAY 15TH

The smell is so bad. I took many showers.

MAY 16TH

Brother is so silly. He was watching a lowbrow comedy show on TV and laughing. I don't like noisy programs like that. I just like to be alone with Brother, in the quiet, reading a book. That is my wish.

MAY 17TH

Let's go to the sea, Brother. You love the sea, right?

MAY 18TH

It's still May, but it's hot, so I asked Brother for some ice cream. How could he bring me back red bean ice cream, though, of all things? Brother doesn't understand at all. I would have been happier with chocolate.

MAY 19TH

I don't like the heat. That's why I don't really wear much.

Do you know what Brother said when he saw me, though? "You look lewd."

He said that! He sounded so indecent when he said it, you see. I've never seen him so frantic in his life. Heheh. I look "lewd" to Brother, don't I? For some reason, that makes me very happy.

MAY 20TH

Why doesn't Brother drive his car very much these days? Does he no longer like driving, I wonder?

MAY 21ST

So many bugs.

MAY 22ND

Let's go to the sea, Brother. You love the sea, right?

"What the hell?" I could feel a chill run down my spine as I read the diary.

At first glance, it was normal, and kind of cute. That's what made it so hard to look at.

Because...

When these entries were written, the brother that was buying her ice cream and watching TV shows was already dead.

I took off my glasses and rubbed my eyes with my fingers.

What most interested me was a phrase that kept showing up in the diary. "Let's go to the sea, Brother. You love the sea, right?" Did that mean something?

I copied it and pasted it into a Google search. I wasn't even sure what I was expecting to find. But...

"Oh." I found something.

There were two sites that matched the phrase in the diary exactly. One of them was the Facebook page I was reading right now. And the other was...

"Kirikiri...Basara?" The exact same phrase was found in the comment section of this aggregator site. And not just once. It was on every article.

I gasped when I saw the dates. The most recent entry was—

"J-just yesterday..."

222. Anonymous Tells It Like It Is
| "Let's go to the sea, Brother. You love the sea, right?"

PARANORMAL SCIENCE NVL.

Occultic;Nine

オカルティック・ナイン

THERE IS NO SUCH THING AS THE "OCCULT." IT CAN ALL BE DISPROVED BY SCIENCE.
ONLY THOSE WHO HAVE ACCEPTED EVERYTHING
HAVE THE RIGHT TO KNOW THE TRUTH.

I was fine. Even in the cold, my hands weren't shaking. I could see the visions, too.

"You're going with your mom. It's already been decided."

When I said that, the voice on the other end of the phone was filled with hope. "If I go with mom, I can be happy, right?"

"I don't know if you'll be happy, I guess. I'm just telling you what I'm seeing. But I did see you eating cake with your mother. I think it was a birthday cake. Your mom was smiling. She looked super happy, and I felt kind of happy looking at her, too."

That was the future of the girl I was talking to on the phone. "My parents are divorcing. I want you to tell me who I'll be happier living with," she'd said, and that was the vision I'd seen.

"Thank you. Now...I can finally make my decision." Evidently, this particular lost puppy had taken my word as a positive. She hung up, sounding relieved.

I let out a small sigh of relief myself, and looked at the window. The curtains were closed, so I couldn't see what was happening outside, but the sun must have already set. It was about 6:20 PM.

After the TV spot, my fortune-telling program was getting absolutely crazy numbers. Over 100,000 people were watching. I'd never had so many people come to watch me.

TV was amazing.

The response was so big, it actually scared me. Thanks to that, I was more nervous than usual. But I'd managed to make it through my first call, and was starting to feel, like, just a little better.

Last time...that guy made me cry. That made me super-frustrated. The video of me sobbing got spread everywhere. I was so embarrassed that I wanted to scream, "Stop it! Just please stop!" When I was finally alone in my house, I did.

Chi suggested we stop for a while, but I'd decided myself to do another episode today. The fact that I'd been on TV didn't really matter. I was doing this stream for the same reason I'd done all the others: to prove that my power wasn't wrong.

So if I could, I wanted to meet the person who'd called me a liar, and see if I'd been wrong. I'd asked for him to contact me when the broadcast started, but...who knew if he would? He hadn't so far.

Chi made me some hot milk tea and set it right where I could reach it. I grabbed the cup and took a sip. It was warm, and helped me relax. The cold started to go away. This room only had a single gas stove, so it never got very warm.

I winked a little to Chi in gratitude. *Thank you.* I could only keep doing this because she was here. That's how super-important Chi was to me.

"All right, let's hear from our next little lost puppy!"

The phone had started ringing before I started to talk, though.

"Stop calling before I tell you to! I won't pick it up!" I waved to the camera as I spoke.

Was I smiling right? I didn't look tense or anything, did I?

I took a deep breath...and I picked up the ringing phone. I was fine. I was just fine.

"Yes, hello. This is Niconico Live Fortune-Telling! Welcome, little lost puppy. Can you give me your name?"

I could hear their breathing on the other side of the phone. It was probably a male caller. Were they not talking because they were nervous? Or...

I gulped.

"Sarai." A calm voice came from the speaker.

Suddenly the screen flooded with comments.

"Sarai's here!"

"The battle we've all been waiting for!"

"No time to eat!"

"Myu-tan, run away!"

"Sarai actually came? Lol"

"Myu, just ignore this guy."

"Myu, hang up the phone!"

"Huh?" Was this Sarai...*that* Sarai? I had a bad feeling about this. Did he call just to start a fight, like the last guy? Should I hang up? But then, I wouldn't be able to see if my power worked.

"Do you know why the fortune-tellers you see on the street don't make any money? Do you know how many of them are poor, Myu?"

"Huh?" Sarai opened up by talking like a teacher at school. I almost began to panic. I had no idea what he was talking about.

This was a fortune-telling stream. People called in and I told their fortunes. That's how it always worked. But Sarai started talking about something that had nothing to do with any of that.

"It's difficult for most fortune-tellers to make their money just by fortune-telling. I personally researched ten fortune-tellers. I'm not including those who use the I Ching here, by the way. And almost all of them said that they do something else in addition to fortune-telling. Do you know what this means?"

"Huh? Wh-what?"

A lot of commenters were telling me to just hang up on him. But Sarai wasn't creepy or scary like the last guy, and he was talking in a normal tone of voice. He wasn't just going to start yelling at me. Well, probably. So I decided to talk to him a little more.

"Use of the I Ching is fundamentally unlike fortune-telling. It's closer to a branch of statistics, actually. They use a vast amount of data to suggest a direction to follow. Fortune-telling is different."

"*Umm...* it is?"

"Yes. Fortune-tellers don't realize the contradiction inherent in their own existence. It's actually quite jocular, isn't it?"

"Jocular..." What did that word mean again?

"If fortune-tellers can see the future, why aren't they able to make a living off that alone? If they needed to, they could just tell their own fortune and choose whatever path would make them successful. They have the power to see the future of others, and change their lives in a positive direction, several times a day. At least, that's what they tell everyone. So it should be no problem, right?"

At this point, I got what he was trying to say.

"But the reason they don't is that fortune-telling doesn't actually reveal the future."

His voice was calm and steady. He was the exact opposite of the guy who called in last time. I looked down at my hands. *I'm fine.*

"I'm...fine," I whispered to myself. My hands balled into tight fists. I acted like I wasn't scared.

I looked at the screen and saw that the commenters were starting to get pissed off.

"Sarai can suck it."

"Let somebody who actually wants their fortune told talk to Myu."

"Some people believe in fortune-tellers, you know!"

"Shut up, faggot."

"Don't be mean to Myu!"

"No one gives a shit."

"Go back to Kirikiri, shithead."

"Nobody wants to see a farce where you fight Myu. Leave!"

I was glad they were on my side, but...*maybe I should tell them not to fight?* At this rate, they were just going to provoke each other, and things would only get worse.

But before I could say something, Sarai responded to the comments from the other side of the phone. "Yes, that's right. This is all a farce. I didn't want to make a big deal out of this, but the commenters at Kirikiri Basara provoked me until I had no choice but to call. But what Myu's doing is no better. Anybody who truly believes that fortune-telling is real should change their mind."

There was too much distracting noise. I bit my lip and gazed at what was going on in front of me. The screen was filled with comments attacking Sarai for his response. There were so many scrolling across that you could barely see my face on the stream.

And Sarai was no better. He was still picking fights with individual commenters. What was going on? I couldn't stop the comments from going out of control. It felt like this was out of my hands now.

Several months ago, when I'd started this stream, there were barely any viewers. I loved that easygoing, relaxed atmosphere. There was nobody to tell me how great I was, or to insult me. People would just watch me, listen to my fortunes, and tell me what they thought.

Was there no way to go back to that now?

But...

But, you know?

"I'm sure—" I opened my mouth. I took off my hood. "I'm sure you're a little lost puppy too, Sarai."

I started to line up my cards like usual. I wasn't even sure what kind of fortune I was trying to tell.

"Hmph. I'm... I'm not lost." I could hear him laughing at me. That pissed me off!

But...had his voice changed a little? *Is this the real you?*

I put the ten cards down in the shape of the Tree of Life.

"Open, Yesod!" I flipped over the ninth card.

What did I see?

Suddenly the screen in front of me seemed to fade away.

Everything went black. For a moment, I didn't know where I was. I heard a voice in my head that wasn't mine.

"Why did you have to get killed? Who did this?! There was so much I wanted to tell you, and I didn't get the chance. I haven't even talked to you for months. Why did I hate you so much? Come on, say something! Dad..."

That was...Sarai's voice, wasn't it?

"Hurry..."

I thought of my father's face. My father, not Sarai's. He was lying on the ground, his eyes closed and his face pale. He was so thin. He was almost nothing but skin and bones.

I couldn't save my mom, and I couldn't save my dad, either.

Even my friends at school thought I was creepy. Dad was the one person who accepted me. He'd taken pictures of the paintings I'd done for me.

He'd been told that he had cancer, and only had six months to live. I didn't want to accept that, and so I'd used fortune-telling to learn his future. I don't remember which of those two events came first. I just wanted to see a future where he was still alive. If I could, I believed that he would survive.

I did my fortune-telling hundreds of times over a period of days, without eating or even sleeping. I always got the same result. I couldn't save Dad.

Maybe he died because I'd kept seeing that future.

It's because of your fortune-telling!

That wasn't true. Dad wouldn't say that. It was just a delusion I'd created from my own guilt.

"Please, Sarai... You need to talk to your dad. Now."

"Wh-what? Why are you talking about my dad?" The tone of Sarai's voice changed.

"If you want to make up with him, listen carefully to what he has to say."

I want to keep telling fortunes. For my father, who believed in me. For my father, who told me that I had the power to see people's futures, and that it wasn't wrong for me to have it. So no matter what they said about me, or how many times they told me I was wrong, I had to keep doing it.

"There's things you want to say to your dad, right? Now's your only chance! If you don't do it right away, you'll super regret it!"

"Y-you're just saying the same thing all fortune-tellers say. It doesn't mean anything. Or is this a threat? You're trying to make me think about my relatives dying to put me at a disadvantage, aren't you! I... I won't give in to threats!" It was no good. No matter what I said, it wouldn't work unless people believed me.

What was I supposed to do at a time like this? We were connected by the phone, but there was a rift—deeper than the sea—between me and Sarai. Maybe no matter how much I reached out my hand, he wouldn't take it.

Even after I'd been able to see it, too. Even though Sarai had the chance to make up with his dad right now. It was so frustrating that he didn't understand.

It hurt so much.

It was so sad.

"I don't have the power to change fate. You have to do it yourself."

Oh...I can't stop crying.

I was crying again. I looked at the card in my hands through blurry eyes. The Dog-Covered Tower, reversed. In the language of the tarot, that meant...

"Erase everything, and look at yourself."

▶ site 11: MMG

"Did you find the code list?" Takasu, now back in his own room, picked a number out of his call history and dialed it. He spoke as soon as it connected. "Did you find the code list?"

"Not yet."

"Then why are you wasting time calling me?" He grabbed a bottle of wine off the shelf and started to pop the cork, the phone still at his ear. "I don't need progress reports. Hang up and get to work. We need to learn its location, and *now*. If that list leaks, it won't just be your responsibility. It may delay the whole plan. And if that happens, who knows how upset our leader will be? You know what that means, right?"

"I... I'm sorry, sir! I'll get the information, no matter what!"

The cork popped at the exact instant the phone call ended. Takasu poured the red wine into a glass and took a sip, enjoying the taste.

The plan couldn't be allowed to collapse because of this. It must all be dealt with in secret—and declared part of the occult.

But...

He swirled the glass in his hand and tilted his head. "Something's not right. Who's behind him?"

▶ site 12: Yuta Gamon ──── 2/17 (Wednesday)

[Breaking News] Sarai gets his ass kicked by Myu Aikawa lololol [Myu-Pom]

From the last episode of "Myu's Niconico Live Fortune-Telling"

■NEET God

SARAI YOU LOSSSSEEEEEE!

You started off great, but then halfway through you started to get wrecked. Apologize to Myu-Pom, seriously.

From now on, Kirikiri Basara will be siding with Myu Aikawa.

(Yeah, baby!)

156: Anonymous's #1 Fan

God you guys are freaking out. Never change.

157: Anonymous's #1 Fan

All I saw was Myu Aikawa crying twice in a row. Someone tell me why we're making it sound like Sarai lost.

158: Anonymous's #1 Fan

Let's go to the sea, Brother. You love the sea, right?

159: Anonymous's #1 Fan

Hey, Sarai! Hey, Sarai!

How'd it feel to lose to a teenage fortune-teller? Huh? How's it feel?

160: Anonymous's #1 Fan

So when's Sarai going to comment about this? I haven't seen him show up once since yesterday. Oh... I know why.

161: Tokotoko

That's a fun stream, huh?

162: Anonymous's #1 Fan

>157

Last time Myu cried because the other guy made her look like a fake. This time that didn't happen.

163: Anonymous's #1 Fan

>157

This time she cried out of pity for Sarai, see. Something about his dad, remember? She's so kind. And so cute.

164: Anonymous's #1 Fan

Guys don't be such dicks to Sarai, lol

He called in to represent us, right? rofl

I stared at the screen. The browser was displaying yesterday's "Myu's Niconico Live Fortune-Telling." I'd seen it live, and then gone back and watched it five times.

I didn't really care about what had happened with Sarai. What was more interesting was...

"Myu-Pom's face really is the cutest!" The way she'd taken off her hood and held herself tight while she silently cried was the cutest thing I'd seen in years. She was a goddess! I was in love.

I'd liked it when she'd cried in frustration the episode before, too, but...

The way she'd cried this time, like she was trying to not let anyone know she was doing it...

"It's just wonderful. A girl's tears are a wonderful thing."

"Gamota, how many times have you said that today?" Master Izumin was looking at me and sighing.

"*Hmph.* I'm sure my feelings are too delicate for you to understand, Master Izumin. For an unpopular NEET boy like me, even tears of sympathy are something I'm insanely jealous of. My conclusion: Sarai can go to hell. Screw him."

"Oh my. That's twisted. Maybe I'll give you a free drink out of sympathy for your inability to get girls, then." He winked at me, and a cold chill ran down my back.

"S-stop it." He was planning on using me as a guinea pig for some weird drink like he did last time. I was grateful that he let me stay here at Café ☆ Blue Moon, but the last one was so nasty, it almost killed me. The stomach pain was so bad, I almost died.

But maybe he'd read what I'd written and changed the recipe. Maybe.

Maybe that's why he was so confident when he gave me the new drink.

Since I was the one who'd given him the advice, it wouldn't be right to turn it down.

I didn't see any way out of it, so I took the drink he offered me—it looked like dark green vegetable juice—and gulped it down.

"Ghawaghhkk! GAACCK!" The instant it touched my lips, an incredible sourness shot from my mouth to the back of my nose and into my brain. It was so painful, I froze and couldn't move.

"WHAT THE HELL IS THIS?!"

"Seaberry juice. It's supposed to be the most sour juice in the world, but it's healthy, so I got some."

"Why the hell did you *do* that?" Not only did he ignore my advice, he wasn't even the one who made this! I was a fool for expecting anything from him. I swallowed some water and swished it around in my mouth. But the shaking sensation in my brain didn't go away. Tears started to pour out of my eyes.

"He can't help it." Ryotasu put her hand on my shoulder and started to nod.

"I really do feel bad for poor Sarai."

"I-is that what we're talking about?"

"Pohya-yah?" Ryotasu tilted her head.

Evidently, the fact that I was suffering from Master Izumin's awful drink meant nothing to melon girl here. Did that mean Sarai meant more to her than I did?

"Ryotasu, what do you see in a jerk like him? D-does he maybe have something that awakens your motherly instincts?! Grr... damn him!"

"Gamotan, don't cry! If you cry, I'll cry, too!"

"I'm crying because of that pervert Master's awful juice!"

"But weren't you on Sarai's side?"

"Bwee hee hee!" My mouth was still partially paralyzed, so my laugh sounded really funny. "Master Izumin, the man who cannot make a drink to save his life, just said something funny! What made you think I would side with a dickhead like Sarai? I'm on Myu-Pom's side, of course."

"Isn't Sarai from Kirikiri Basara, though?"

Well, sure. The site mostly got by thanks to his comments, but...

"Master Izumin, Sarai is old news now. He's finished! I'm grateful for what he's done for us so far, but after the bitch-slapping Myu-Pom gave him yesterday, things have changed."

"Oh, so you're giving up on him, huh? You're such a cruel man, Gamota."

"Say what you like. But once you look at this, you'll understand." I pulled up a counter on my laptop that showed the total hits Kirikiri Basara had gotten since yesterday.

"Look at this! Ten times more views than yesterday! Ten times! Kirikiri Basara is finally a famous affiliate blog! Oh man, what should I do? I'm gonna get even more haters than before! This is definitely the Myu-Pom Effect! Myu-Pom's got the magic touch! I don't need Sarai! I've got Myu-Pom!" I'd done nothing over the last few days but upload articles about Myu-Pom, and the hit counter had gone up *this* much. The whole internet knew that Kirikiri Basara was the place to go for the latest Myu-Pom information. This was good news.

"Mwaha! I can't wait to see next month's income! I may be able to get you that yogurt soon, Ryotasu!"

"Poya?" Ryotasu was spacing out like always.

Maybe she'd forgotten that she'd told me to buy her some yogurt? That would be kind of depressing.

I rubbed the tears away with the sleeve of my shirt.

"Maybe we should just switch to being a Myu-Pom site. Her fortune-telling is the real thing."

"Huh. You believe in fortune-telling, Gamota?" Master Izumin looked surprised for a moment, but he quickly offered me a copy of *Kyam-Kyam* with a satisfied look on his face. "Read this, then. You want to read your beloved Myu's fortune-telling column, right?"

"Oh, thanks." I decided to accept it gratefully. "W-wait! It's not like I believe in fortune-telling! It's not scientific at all."

I was just interested in the column because Myu-Pom wrote it. "But whatever Myu-Pom does, I'll forgive it. And I'll believe her. Cuteness equals truth, you see."

"Yup, yup. I think so, too!" Oh, wow. Ryotasu actually participated in a conversation for once.

"That's my Ryotasu for you. That's just what I want to see from the staff of Kirikiri Basara." I decided to keep my tears over the yogurt to myself.

"I don't think anybody wants science in their fortune-telling, you know?"

"That's what you call not thinking. That's what wrong-siders do. You can't get by these days if you're like that."

"Is that how it works? What about that one guy? You know, the one on TV with the long hair?"

There were a lot of guys on TV with long hair.

"The famous teacher from your school. He's older, but he's got really long hair, so I can picture his face, but...what was his name? Gama... Gami?"

"It's Dr. Hashigami! ♪ "

"Yeah, that's right! Him!"

Oh, Professor Hashigami, huh? Yeah, he was a professor at Seimei Academy, my school. He worked for the university, not the high school, though. "What about him?"

"Didn't he say recently that he could scientifically prove the existence of ghosts?"

He did. He used to be totally against the occult, but lately, he'd suddenly changed his mind. He'd started saying that he could scientifically prove the existence of ghosts. Not that anyone actually *believed* the guy.

"I don't really like that stuff. All I want from ghosts is for them to show up in haunted houses and horror stories and scare me. I'm sure that's what most people think, right?"

"Sure. I think it's important to have something that adds spice to life." The occult was supposed to be scary. "But Master Izumin, humans are creatures that seek answers."

"Oh my. Aren't you the little showoff?"

"I'm the admin of an occult blog! Even if I don't believe in the occult!" If you could scientifically prove that ghosts were real, that would shake the whole occult industry to its core. You wouldn't be able to make horror movies, either. Even the famous ghost-story teller Mr. Inagawa would go out of business. But even so, humans weren't capable of leaving something that they couldn't explain alone.

I should use that on Kirikiri Basara.

"Hey, hey, Samurai Gamonosuke!" Ryotasu grabbed the hem of my shirt and pulled. "Hey, hey, let's go see Dr. Hashigami!"

"Huh? Why?"

"We can do a story for Kirikiri Basara! It's okay, right, Samurai

Gamonosuke?"

Why was I a samurai, anyway? But...

"I never thought of that. If we did an exclusive interview with Professor Hashigami, it might boost our page views." *He's at the same school I am, so I might as well, right?* "It's a pain in the butt, though. And he's on TV all the time. My honor wouldn't let me just go up and ask him for an interview. Huh, I became a samurai for a moment there. Tee hee!"

I didn't really know that much about the occult. And I knew even less about science. And there was no way a NEET God like me could ask someone who was on TV all the time for an interview. Even if I tried, I'd get scared and run away at the last minute. I hated to say it, but I just wasn't that brave. Just thinking about it was enough to bring back the stomach pain.

"Correspondent Ryotasu!"

"Ponyah? Correspondent?"

"Y-you were the one who came up with the idea, so you go handle the interview! Don't screw it up!"

"Wow! I got a mission! I'll do my best!" Ryotasu raised her hands and jumped around. Each time she landed, her huge breasts shook up and down. Amazing.

"Correspondent! Correspondent! Corres-corres-high-voltage-old-man!" Ryotasu started to sing a strange song that sounded like some kind of curse, but Master Izumin stopped her.

"I'm about to open the shop. My real customers are about to arrive, so can you two leave?" And then we were kicked out of the café.

The clock read 7:00 PM exactly. After sunset, the wind in Kichijoji was cold. I missed being in a heated room.

"Man, I wonder if Myu-Pom is walking around out here. There's a good chance I could run into her." When she'd been on TV, they'd done the filming in Kichijoji, so she definitely lived around here.

Well, if I spent all my time at Café ☆ Blue Moon, I was probably never going to see her. If I wanted to meet a girl like her, I'd have to go to Starbucks or something.

I held my computer with both hands as I walked down the street. The screen was displaying a frozen image of Myu-Pom. I sighed and went to close it, when...

"I know where Myu is." Ryotasu looked up at the sky and spoke without warning.

"Huh? You know where she is?"

"Look, it's right here." Ryotasu turned around and pointed at the screen.

"Here? You know where it is?"

"It's the AV room, right? At your school?"

For a moment, I didn't know what she was saying. I stared at Ryotasu's face.

Then at the laptop screen.

Then I looked back at Ryotasu.

She grinned back at me.

"It's the AV room at your school, right?"

"Huh?! What?!" I hadn't even thought about it until she said it. There was always a good chance that Myu-Pom went to a high school in Kichijoji. But still...could it be?

"Am I... lucky?"

I suddenly felt a presence and froze, my hand above the tablet. I'd been looking into aromatic oils with a mild hypnotic effect.

I took a glance around the shop. After the sun set, the shop was filled with more darkness than the single tiny light could illuminate. It was a small shop, but it was crammed with items I used in my black magic, so there were many parts of it I couldn't see from where I was sitting.

I felt a presence. A presence that projected a deep sensation of evil. But despite the presence's intensity, I couldn't tell if it was behind me, or perhaps in a corner of the shop. It felt strangely uncomfortable.

"Are you there?" I spoke to no one in particular, and the bulb hanging from the ceiling shook a little. It was a freezing cold night already, but it felt like my body temperature had dropped even lower.

I ignored the cold and continued. "You haven't been around much, so I had thought that perhaps you might be busy."

The first response was...

⟨Heheh...⟩

It was an awful breath, like a snort. I could feel it on the back of my neck, and I shivered.

But there was no one behind me. There wasn't room for anyone to stand. All that was behind me was a shelf and my dolls.

The next thing I heard was a man's low voice, like a whisper. ⟨I've had many new customers lately.⟩

No, it only felt to me like a man's voice. Perhaps it wasn't.

"It's good to have a lot of customers," I said.

⟨It's a lousy economy. When you're poor, you don't have any free time, you know?⟩ He was joking, but it was all I could do to hide my nervousness. I could feel sweat building up under my armpits.

That "voice" was not at all easy to hear.

It was muffled, somehow.

But it felt like it went right through your ears and directly into your brain.

There was no way to tell where it was coming from.

And it made you feel very uneasy.

I never could get used to it.

When you listened to the voice, you gradually started to lose your senses of direction and distance.

I yanked a doll off the shelf behind me to try and hide my nervousness. I ended up grabbing Coven. Its goofy-looking, five-eyed face was staring up at me. I held it gently against my stomach.

The thing I was speaking to didn't show itself. But I knew what it was. It was a creature of darkness, feared by man since ancient times, and sometimes worshiped by those who would rebel against God.

It was a devil.

"Why does a devil need money?" This devil had said that it was poor. In that case, it was quite a worldly devil. Of course, that was appropriate enough for a devil.

⟨Hmph. Why ask that now? Did you forget about our contract?⟩

Of course, I hadn't forgotten. Two years ago, the person I loved had died. I'd been left all alone. Just as I'd given in to despair, and was about to step in front of a train, I'd heard this voice in my head.

Death is given to those chosen for it. You have no right to that yet.

And so, I decided not to die.

Ever since then, this devil had been my partner. I didn't do my work as a black magic agent alone. I heard the clients' stories and researched the information, and then this devil carried out their requests.

I gave the devil half the money I earned. That was the contract.

⟨In this place, even mercy can only be earned with money. You know that well, don't you?⟩

"So you have the concept of a bad economy, too, then? But then, why is it always the living who suffer?"

⟨Hey, things aren't exactly a picnic down here, you know? Like that last client... Um, what was it? The screaming package?⟩

Dying Screams. The 42,420 yen package.

⟨Bringing somebody absolute despair ain't exactly easy, you know. When the client's got a strong heart, you should pay me double, honestly.⟩

"And when they're weak, and the job is simple, may I pay you half?"

⟨Heheh...⟩ The devil snorted and fell silent, as if it was unsatisfied.

I'd tried to record this voice once. There was a small trace of this unnerving voice on the recording. It sounded mostly like white noise, but I was able to hear it.

In other words, this devil's voice was neither some form of spiritual telepathy, nor evidence of my own delusion. It was a sound, made by vibrating the air. Even if I couldn't pinpoint the source of the voice, it existed in this space as a vibration of the air.

"When humans are born, they realize their misery and cry. And from then on, their hearts keep getting weaker and weaker. You just give their weak heart a little push. For you, that's an easy job, right?" Of course, I was suspicious as to whether or not this devil was actually doing his job.

I'd never gone and checked. And no one had ever come back to complain, or thank me. Whether that was a good thing or a bad thing, it felt like if I dug any deeper, my relationship with this devil would come to an end.

⟨Tell me about the new jobs.⟩

Either way, I was a woman who'd sold her soul to a devil. Maybe the real reason I deposited the money in the account the devil gave me was just to make myself feel better. It was my way of making the devil shoulder half the guilt I felt for earning money off other people's misery. So, from my perspective, it didn't matter whether he did the jobs or not.

"Isayuki Hashigami."

⟨Heheh... Well, how about that?⟩

In addition to the bloody mass of hair I'd found in my mailbox yesterday, there was also an envelope containing 66,600 yen. The payment had been made. I didn't know who the client was, but I no longer had any reason to refuse.

"Please perform the Devil's Ritual." Since ancient times, it has always been those who turn their backs on God that choose who will be sacrificed to the Devil.

⟨Put it in my usual account.⟩

That's when my conversation with the devil usually ended. The presence would disappear, and the air in the shop would return to normal. That's what had always happened so far. I had no particular interest in making small talk with my devil.

But this time, for some reason, I asked him a question. "May I ask you something?"

⟨Huh? Depends on what you ask. This is a business, you know. There's some things I can't tell you, some things I don't want to tell you, and some things you don't want to know. Right?⟩ The devil spoke back to me. He always did like to talk. One word for him might be "garrulous."

"If the target of a curse is already dead, is it possible for someone to get their money back?"

⟨Heheh…⟩ The devil didn't answer.

I became even more anxious and kept talking. "All the black magic requires is a few strands of hair. But this client was different. They brought me a whole lump of his hair. It felt like they were obsessed."

The hair was so creepy that I wanted to throw it away, but I couldn't. So I'd put it in a trash bag and thrown it onto the back of the shelf.

"If they took that much of the target's hair, isn't it possible that they died before you can carry out the curse?"

⟨So that's why you asked about getting their money back? That's funny.⟩ Once again, the devil didn't answer. Instead the light bulb flashed again.

The awful presence seemed to subside, somewhat. Maybe.

⟨Hold on a second. Someone's outside.⟩

Outside? Did he mean down the stairs?

⟨It doesn't look like a customer. It's a short man in a beige trench coat.⟩

I had no idea who it could be, so I wasn't sure what to say.

⟨He looks like a kid, but the way he moves makes me suspicious. *Tch.* He got away. Anyway, time for me to go, too. See you around.⟩ This time, the evil presence disappeared. I thought I heard the front door shake a little, but it was probably just a draft.

I had not the slightest intention of going down the stairs to look for the man in the coat.

I never checked to see if the devil was doing his job. I never fully believed what he told me. That was how I kept myself sane.

"How ugly this must be..." I palmed Coven's head as it rested on my lap and crushed it with my hand. I suddenly realized I was very thirsty.

"So, how's the new plan going?"

Takasu displayed an email on the men's tablets in answer to Hatoyama's question. It was a picture of tiny numbers marked with explanatory diagrams.

"The spectrum diffusion experiments were a success," Takasu replied, "and we've succeeded in improving the accuracy of the communications."

The sitting men responded positively.

"The Scandium project is proceeding nicely. We're performing monitoring tests on all subjects from the first to third generations, and they're all reporting normal values. All their thought patterns are normal."

"How does it compare to the RFID microchips?" one man asked.

"There's no comparison. Input, output, and communication accuracy are around ten times greater than they were before."

"I've received some reports of problems, however. Are they true?" asked someone else.

Takasu's smile didn't waver for an instant. "It's true that there have been bugs."

"You've got to be kidding me." Matoba began to rise from his chair. "Is everything okay? I don't want a repeat of the problems with the microchips."

"There are no problems whatsoever," Takasu said. His glance froze Matoba in place. "None at all."

There was a certain pitch and rhythm achievable by the human voice that could induce sleep in others.

Professor Takaoka, the man currently giving a lecture to fifty or so students, was most likely unaware of this. But still, he was better than anyone else at this school when it came to putting people to sleep.

I thought about that as I looked around the lecture hall. There were a lot of students lying facedown on their desks. About 60% of them were asleep.

It was the last lecture of the year, and next week, finals began. Passing those finals was supposed to be every student's top priority, so it was fair to call the whole lot of them slackers.

Professor Takaoka was ignoring them and continuing his lecture on economics. It was a boring class. I'd realized it when I'd heard his first lecture in the course about a year ago.

Right after the school year had started, I'd been annoyed that even after making it into the School of Science and Engineering, I still had to take classes on unrelated subjects. But that was the system and there was no helping it.

Over the course of the last year, I'd taken a few more classes than I should, so I'd earned quite a few credits.

I'd heard that in your second and third years, you spent a lot of time doing experiments with your seminar class. So Dad had told me that even if it meant doing some extra work, I should take a lot of credits my first year.

It felt like the professor was occasionally glancing in my direction, which made it hard to relax. In the past hour, he'd looked at me no less than sixteen times. Over the past year of taking his lectures, I'd gotten the feeling that he wasn't the type to look at people when he talked, so it felt strange.

I thought that perhaps there was something stuck on my face, but since the other students were all ignoring me, that didn't seem to be the case. Either way, it was upsetting me, so I decided to pretend I wasn't listening and look down at the smartphone in my hand.

I groaned a little without even realizing I was doing it. I tried to analyze my own mental state to see where this frustration was coming from.

Was it Professor Takaoka's rude glances? Was it frustration at my own stupidity for asking Dad for advice on my class schedule a year ago? Or—

Was it because of the affiliate blog I was looking at on my smartphone?

The LCD screen was displaying a blog called Kirikiri Basara. I commented there often under the nickname "Sarai." I could've used my full name, Sarai Hashigami, but there were idiots out there who knew nothing about internet decency, and who would try to show up in your real life. I didn't want them showing up at my doorstep, so I just used a nickname.

All the stories on Kirikiri Basara were *extremely* stupid, but the sheer illogic of them all pissed me off, and I spent a lot of time giving the idiots there scientific lectures.

But now...

They were saying I'd lost. How could anyone be that stupid? But even the site admin was joining in. If I'd known this was going to happen, I never would've called into Myu Aikawa's program. I hadn't intended to in the first place. The people at Kirikiri Basara had provoked me.

I tapped my phone to open the comment entry box on Kirikiri Basara. I'd decided to write back at the people who were insulting me.

"Wow." A male student next to me, whose name I didn't know, watched the movements of my fingers with a stupid look on his face. I glared at him as I adjusted my glasses, and he grinned feebly before he looked away.

He was probably surprised at how fast I was typing, but I wasn't here to show off.

I'd been using my smartphone for five or six years now. I'd gotten used to flick input. There was no way I could go back to the Japanese-style phones I'd used in elementary school. Not that I had any intention of trying.

I looked back at the screen and continued typing my response. If I walked them through this logically, step by step, it was probably going to take a long time. But I didn't care.

I was trying to explain things to the kind of useless idiots who believed in occult things like fortune-telling. I couldn't help but make it long.

But idiots wouldn't read a long post. This was a dilemma. It was hard, dealing with idiots.

The only sound in the big lecture hall was Professor Takaoka's voice.

I resisted the urge to shout, and instead, I deleted the entire comment instead of uploading it. I'd been like this ever since my argument with Myu Aikawa two days ago. I'd write something, then delete it, then write something else and delete it again. I hadn't managed to post a single comment.

It felt like no matter what I wrote now, it would come off like an excuse. No matter how right I was, it felt like they'd just make fun of me. If I could just meet them in person for a debate, I could shut them up within a minute—

"You there." Professor Takaoka was talking to someone from his podium.

The boy next to me was still staring at me. The girl sitting in front turned backward to look at me. I could hear the other students chuckling, too.

I looked up and saw that Professor Takaoka was pointing at me. "Is my lecture so boring that you feel the need to play with your phone?"

That was strange. I'd reached the conclusion that Professor Takaoka was the kind of person who wouldn't interrupt a lecture no matter how many students slept or did other things. Was I wrong? No, that was impossible.

So maybe he had it out for me for some reason? And this was his way of getting at me? "Let's see if you were paying attention. Point out the central issues here."

He motioned toward the blackboard. On the board was written a summary of Keynesian economic theory.

I sighed and stood up. "First, in a situation of underemployment where involuntary employment exists, national income and the level of employment are decided by effective demand, which is the sum of consumption and investment. Second, an increase in investment can result in a gain in income greater than the investment itself. Third, interest is the price one is paid for a loss of liquidity, and the interest rate is to be adjusted to achieve a balance between the demand for highly liquid cash assets and the supply of currency."

"Mm... Mmmh?"

"The inevitable result of these three propositions is that the government should enact policies to stimulate investment and consumption demand—"

Professor Takaoka started to cough like there was something in his throat.

The answer I'd given was word-for-word out of an encyclopedia. I was only interested in science and engineering, and didn't see much point in seriously studying economics. A copy-and-paste job was good enough for me.

But the professor seemed astonished at my answer. It was pretty funny. It was stupid, actually.

"What is it?"

"No, if you were listening, that's fine." He backed down a lot more easily than I thought he would. Now it was my turn to be surprised.

"Even if you think it's fine, I don't."

Professor Takaoka's eyes went wide when I spoke. I could hear the other students' laughter change to murmurs of confusion. They probably hadn't thought I'd say anything back to him.

"Why only come after me? There are other students sleeping or playing with their phones who are being much more obvious than I am." For example, some were wearing flashier clothes or sitting in more visible locations. I'd deliberately chosen to sit in the part of the room that made me least likely to be noticed.

"I just happened to see you playing with your phone. That's all." I didn't miss the tone of annoyance in his voice.

"I don't know why, but you seem slightly irritated. For example, there were signs of it when the lecture started. It's safe to assume that it's the result of a series of small irregularities that occurred before the lecture began."

"What did you say?" He seemed confused as I pointed this out.

But I kept talking anyway. "You're always very particular about your appearance, but today, you're wearing the same necktie as yesterday. This is likely because you were running short on time, and had no choice but to grab the closest one available. As for why I know what kind of necktie you were wearing yesterday, that's not really a serious issue. I happened to see you then. And when I did, I remember I laughed at your terrible taste in neckties. I was actually astonished to see you wearing the same awful tie two days in a row."

"Grr... Now listen, you..." His face was flushed with anger, but he hesitated for a moment as he thought about whether it was right for a teacher to scream at one of his students.

I kept talking before he could finish making his decision. "The necktie indicates that you were almost late for the lecture. You even forgot the atomic watch you always wear, the one with the leather strap. Three times during the lecture you've looked at your left arm, expecting to find it."

The professor looked at his left arm in shock. Of course, the watch wasn't there.

"Since you were in such a hurry this morning, professor, you didn't eat breakfast. That's caused your blood sugar levels to drop. The effects of this are obvious. Sixty-four minutes into the lecture, your stress levels began to rapidly rise. That was just when you decided to relieve your stress by hassling me." I could tell the other students were listening to me in shock.

I didn't care about them, nor was I interested in making a speech like this, but whenever you wanted to explain something logically, it always ended up taking a long time. It wasn't like any of them were paying attention to the lecture anyway. None of them would care if I wasted a few more minutes.

"So the question then becomes, why did you oversleep this morning? By the way, when I saw you yesterday, it wasn't on campus, it was in front of Kichijoji Station. You were heading with a group of friends into Harmonica Alley. This was at 9:19 PM."

The students were murmuring to themselves.

I shrugged my shoulders a little. "I have no particular interest in your drinking habits. It wasn't like you were drinking during lecture, after all. It's not a problem. But because you drank too much, you overslept, and you were almost late for lecture. I'm very nearly certain of this."

The professor had a bitter look on his face, but he didn't say anything. It was safe to assume that I was right.

"But why take your frustration out on me, then? During the sixty-four minutes before you called on me, our eyes met sixteen times. The first time, you made two glances at me, for a full total of seventeen times, but we can disregard that. Averaged out, our eyes met once every four minutes. There are around fifty students in this lecture hall. I represent only one-fiftieth of the total number of students, but you looked at me no fewer than sixteen times. I haven't done the exact math, but the odds of that seem far too low for it to be a coincidence."

"It's a coincidence. A meaningless number." The professor was mumbling in a tiny voice as he looked away from me.

"You just put your left hand into your pocket, didn't you?"

"Wh-what?" It seemed he'd only realized that after I'd pointed it out to him.

"When a person is caught off-guard, they'll try to protect their left side, where their heart is. You may think that's meaningless, but from a psychological perspective, it's not. I wouldn't consider myself an expert at psychology, but I'm told that when someone tries to hide the fact that they're lying, they attempt to protect their left side, where their heart is found. Of course, that's just one theory among many." But what was important here wasn't the psychological reasoning. "More importantly, did you realize that during the entire lecture, you've been putting your left hand into your pocket to touch something inside of it?"

The professor said nothing.

"There's no bulge in your pocket, so I'm sure it's paper. A memo or something. Did you see the list of seminars for the next year that was handed out yesterday? Most of the popular teachers' seminars are already full. But what about yours?"

I could see the color draining from his face. It was probably due to his mental state.

"If you're concerned about your popularity, try not to get so frustrated. And certainly don't attempt to take your frustration out on a student. It's embarrassing."

"I... I don't understand what you're getting at. And I don't think it's appropriate for you to speak this way to your elder. Students these days... Enough." The professor shrugged and turned away from me, then began writing more text on the blackboard.

I guess in the end, he never admitted to it. But there was no way it was a coincidence that he'd come after me. He hadn't said it, but I knew.

It was because I was Isayuki Hashigami's son, wasn't it? He didn't have it out for me, personally. When he looked at me, he didn't see me, he saw Isayuki Hashigami.

The reason was the memo in his left pocket. It was a list of next year's seminar classes. The popular seminars were already flooded with requests, and in some cases, you couldn't get in at all.

That didn't seem to be the case for Takaoka's seminar, but it certainly was for Hashigami's. All the students, not just me, knew that Takaoka had it out for Isayuki Hashigami.

Isayuki Hashigami was on TV all the time and everyone knew who he was. It was easy to think of him as a bit of a playboy. Professor Takaoka, by contrast, was a very dull man. He probably didn't like that. But it was a mistake to try and take his frustrations out on me.

The silence of the classroom and the stares of the other students were starting to annoy me. The lecture wasn't over, but I got my things together and left. I might not get credit for the class, but I didn't care. One single lost credit wasn't going to hurt me.

I left Building #3, where the lecture hall was located. Outside, it was drizzling, and the air was so cold that I shivered. The rain had started late last night, and showed no signs of letting up today.

I put up my umbrella and ran across the courtyard called the Atrio. The area was filled with greenery centered around a big keyaki tree, and it was typical on sunny days to see students sitting here and talking.

But, thanks to the weather, there was nobody here today, and the deserted atmosphere made it feel hard to breathe. I headed for the bulletin board at the side of the courtyard.

Seimei University, the school I attended, was about fifteen minutes' walk from Kichijoji Station. There were fourteen classroom buildings, a cutting-edge library, a gym, a track, a student building, a café, and other buildings scattered about the campus. In addition to the four departments and ten specialties in Seimei University's School of Science and Engineering, there were also attached elementary, middle, and high schools. The name "Seimei Academy" encompassed all these schools together.

Exams started next week at the university. The bulletin boards were filled with notices about the exams and next year's seminars. I went through each of them to see if they had anything to do with me.

"Oh..." My eyes stopped when I saw a paper with a certain name on it.

It was a notice that Professor Hashigami's seminar for the day was canceled. Jeez... Talk about irony.

I wasn't in that seminar myself.

Isayuki Hashigami...

The country's leading occult researcher and a man who was on TV all the time. A professor at the Seimei University School of Science and Engineering. And...my dad.

How long had it been since I'd last talked to him? We lived in the same house, but I barely even saw him anymore. He was busy with work—TV work, not his university job—and was spending less and less time at home.

He'd always been something of a showoff, and he was a good conversationalist. You could tell how popular he was from the sheer number of students that wanted to take his classes.

There were so many that even the middle school kids at Seimei were talking about it. I'd actually heard the rumors when I was in middle school myself, so I knew that for a fact.

So when I'd heard he'd declared his belief in the occult, at first, I'd thought he was just doing it to show off. I was annoyed, but didn't really think much else of it. But once I'd understood that he was going on TV and really trying to prove that the occult was real, I became disgusted with him as a scientist.

Prove the existence of the occult scientifically? That was impossible. You'd have to be an idiot to try.

Did he know how many people had tried it in the past? Every one of them had failed and become a laughingstock in the scientific community. I didn't want to admit that my dad could be so stupid.

Not that I had any idea what brought this on. I'd respected my dad as a scientist. I'd come this far because I wanted to do the same research he did. That's why I'd felt betrayed.

Please, Sarai. You need to talk to your dad. Now.

I remembered the sorrow in Myu Aikawa's words. I gripped the handle of my umbrella tighter.

Just standing here, it felt like the cold from the asphalt was climbing up my legs. My wet toes were starting to go numb. *I should just go home,* I thought. I didn't even want to think about my dad. I wasn't scheduled to work at my part-time job today, so I could get some hot menchi-katsu at Meat Satou before I got home.

Suddenly, I heard the faint sound of clinking metal. And then I realized that there was a brilliant blue covering the right side of my field of vision.

A woman carrying an umbrella was standing right next to me. The blue was her umbrella and I couldn't see her face because of it.

I hadn't noticed her at all, so my heart rate accelerated in shock. I was just barely able to keep from flinching away.

I didn't want to embarrass myself like I did on the stream. I adjusted my glasses and calmed myself down as I took a look at her.

She was looking at the bulletin board like I was... maybe. But I couldn't understand why she would stand so close. Did she realize that the water was dripping off her umbrella and onto my shoulder?

I couldn't see her face, but it was obvious enough from the shape of her body, and the fluffy coat and muffler she was wearing, that she was a woman. She stood tall, like a statue.

Did I know her? I'd been going to this academy since elementary school, so I knew a lot of the other students. I didn't consider any of them my friends, but if I passed by them on campus, I could at least say hello.

I heard the clinking sound again. There was a distinctive golden necklace shining on her chest. Three small bars hung down from an upside-down triangle shape, and whenever they struck each other, they made a small, pleasant noise.

A triangle and three bars.

Three was recognized as an important number worldwide. For instance, there was the concept of the Christian Trinity. Some people said it was a holy number.

And hers was upside down... There was a mark like an eyeball on the upside-down triangle. It was one I'd seen somewhere before. But I couldn't immediately remember where. It seemed like something that was really famous, though.

As I was thinking about it, the woman shifted her umbrella's position. Suddenly, I couldn't look away from her. She was a very beautiful woman.

Her long black hair was just the slightest bit curly, and her eyes were sad beneath her long eyelashes. Her lips seemed soft. Everything about her looked glossy, as if she were wet.

I thought that she might have been standing in the rain without an umbrella for a long time, but since her clothes weren't wet, maybe I was just imagining it. Either way, I'd never been so struck by a girl like this in my life. I was shocked to see how much I was freaking out.

My heart rate refused to slow down. My sympathetic nerves were on fire. It was clear that this woman was the cause.

She seemed older than me, but I didn't recognize her face. When I realized that, I suddenly felt extremely embarrassed. It was like I was a tiny little child next to her.

I quickly turned to go, and my eyes met with hers. I almost forgot to breathe.

"Looks like it's canceled, huh?" she whispered in a calm voice, totally unlike the idiot girls my age.

I wasn't sure if she was talking to me, or to herself, so I wasn't sure if I should respond.

"Did the devil eat him? Or—" She sounded just the slightest bit excited, and just the slightest bit mischievous.

And just the slightest bit teasing.

"Or is it about to eat him?" I thought I heard her whisper in my ear.

Her voice was so soft that it seemed like it would be drowned out by the tiny drizzle of rain. But I could hear it clearly.

She winked at me as I stood there in shock, and walked away, spinning her umbrella. All I could do was watch.

"Eaten by a devil? What does that mean?" By the time I was finally able to speak, the blue umbrella was gone.

PARANORMAL SCIENCE NVL
Occultic;Nine

THERE IS NO SUCH THING AS THE "OCCULT." IT CAN ALL BE DISPROVED BY SCIENCE.
ONLY THOSE WHO HAVE ACCEPTED EVERYTHING
HAVE THE RIGHT TO KNOW THE TRUTH.

There's no such thing as a devil, right? If anything in the world deserved the name "devil," it would be the human heart.

The darkness within the human heart ran deep. Everyone possessed that darkness, and everyone loved that darkness.

That sounded a little poetic, so I laughed to myself as I spun my favorite blue umbrella. I was feeling a little happy, probably because of the cute young man in glasses I'd just run into at the university. I should have asked for his name.

I thought these things to myself as I walked through Inokashira Park in the rain. It was a weekday afternoon in the middle of winter, so the place would've been pretty empty otherwise. With the rain, almost no one was here.

I walked through the silent park with my blue umbrella, feeling at peace, like I'd wandered into a fantasy world. The Natural Culture Gardens, a zoo inside the park grounds, was a particular favorite of mine. It had an aquarium, too, and the fact that it was surrounded by trees made it feel isolated from the rest of the world.

Sometimes you could hear the cries of the ducks and cranes in their cages. Just watching the waterfowl round themselves up into little balls in the rain was enough to make me want to stand there for hours.

It had been almost a year since they'd told me that my mind was broken. Of course, I liked to think I could tell the difference between real and unreal, but I had nothing to prove that what I was seeing was actually real at all.

Since there was no way to prove that life was anything but a dream, that was only natural. Still, if that was the case, I wanted the things I saw to at least seem a little fantastic. Maybe that's why I came here whenever it rained.

"Um..." My enjoyment was unexpectedly interrupted.

It was a girl I didn't know, about my age, who had spoken to me.

"Are you Ririka Nishizono?"

"Yes." I was able to smile back in a very natural manner.

If someone had spoken to me outside this park, I would've ignored them or spat at them. But this was a place where I could be calm. I could treasure my meeting with this person.

"I knew it! The rumors were true!" The woman got excited when she saw me nod.

"I saw it on Twitter! That you go to Inokashira Park when it's raining." I'd been spoken to several times before when walking through the park. I wondered how they realized who I was when I wasn't anyone famous. That must have been why. Of course, if someone had to speak to me in town, I'd much rather they did it here.

"I also heard that if I asked for a sketch, you'd give me one. Is that true?"

"I don't have my sketchbook with me."

"No, um... I brought one." She hesitated a little as she took a sketchbook out of her bag.

Oh my. She was certainly prepared.

"Certainly." I was something of a manga artist, after all.

I hadn't gone pro yet, but I'd published several amateur doujinshi that had sold quite well. If nothing else, they were popular enough that people talked about me on the internet.

It was a little disappointing that it was always girls who approached me, however. I would've preferred a cute younger man. If that ever happened, I would seduce him into coming home with me, and then show him a world that he never dreamed existed.

I imagined that and shuddered.

"What kind of picture would you like?"

"Um... I'd like something from your book at last year's Winter Comiket, *The Bottom of the Deep Water*. When the albino boy is doing, um... naughty things...to the twins at the shrine, and they're liking it."

"Heheh. You know exactly what you want, don't you?" She must have dreamed of the day she'd meet me, and spent a lot of time fantasizing about the sketch she wanted.

When I asked her if she had, she looked at the ground in embarrassment.

In the rain, holding my umbrella, I was drawing BL sketches in an empty zoo. It was a romantic and erotic act.

I didn't labor under the delusion that my art was very good. My failure to go pro had proven its inadequacy.

But whenever I met a fan, they always told me that my art excited them. That must have been what made my drawings special.

Not that I really understood, myself. My own sexual proclivities were relatively normal. I only ever thought about sweet love between men when I was working. There were many female artists out there who imagined things far more extreme than I ever did.

That's why I was surprised to find that I had so many fans.

I was a fast artist. I always drew these pictures very quickly, without expending any real effort. I wanted to make it so the person who asked me to draw for them could fill in the blanks with their own minds.

I finished quickly, relying on the first image that came into my head. After only three minutes or so, I handed the girl back her finished picture.

And then I realized...

There was someone else, standing some distance away. He was looking right at me.

"Wow, this is wonderful! I love it! I'll treasure it forever!"

"Thank you very much." I'd forgotten all about my happy fan.

My mind, my senses, my self...my everything had been captured by the person staring at me.

He was a young boy, about middle school age, like a character from the sketch I'd just drawn. But his expression was far too empty for someone of that age. He had a different air about him than the boy with glasses I'd seen at the school.

You could say...yes, he was identical. He was identical to the albino boy in my books.

"Has God made my dream come true, perhaps?" I whispered in a tiny voice.

The rumors I'd heard said that God appeared in Inokashira Park.

Even after my fan had finished saying her thanks and left, the young boy didn't move. He was standing still in the rain, without even an umbrella.

I walked over to him and put my umbrella over his wet head. I could smell a strong sweat coming from him. It made me feel warm in the center of my body.

"You'll catch cold." The boy didn't look away from me, even when I was right in front of him.

No one had ever stared at me like this before.

"The story you wrote was pretty good." He took off his backpack and took out one of my books.

"That's a naughty book for girls. Why do you have it?" I asked, wanting to tease him.

Normally, a boy his age would've blushed or gotten embarrassed. But there was no particular change to the boy's expression. Instead, he kept looking directly into my eyes. His eyes were so clear, like a doll's, that I...

"Your eyes are so pretty." I imagined that they were drawing me in. "Did you know that the eyes don't feel pain? That's why it's okay to lick them."

I was aroused. I wanted to take this innocent young boy with me and teach him to be exactly what I wanted.

I softly ran my thumb down his lips, which had turned blue from the chill. They were so cold. My heart shivered.

"I'm a minor. If I buy one of your books, is that a crime? I'm fine, right? Maybe I'm not supposed to do it, but they won't arrest me, right?" The boy offered me his book. "Draw me a box, please."

For a moment, I didn't know what he meant. "A box?" That was a strange request.

He didn't want a character or an autograph. He wanted a box. How cute.

"Will you tell me your name, too?" I asked, intending to dedicate the picture to him.

The boy answered, still expressionless. "Sagami."

"That's a good name. I could just eat it up." The pendant on my chest clinked.

But young Sagami looked straight at me, still expressionless. I wasn't hoping for an expression, either.

That sounded a little poetic, so I laughed to myself as I spun my favorite blue umbrella. This was the most erotic expression he could have made in this scene.

"So what kind of box shall I draw?"

The boy moved his mouth and nothing else, like a ventriloquist's doll.

"A kotoribako," he said.

A child-stealing box.

It happened on a summer day half a year ago. I was sitting alone on a bench in Kichijoji Park like always, playing with my Skysensor. I didn't expect to hear more than the usual white noise, but I was spinning the tuner anyway, mostly out of habit. But that day, I heard a noise that was just a little different.

PYUUUIJJJZZ... CHA...TA...

I was so excited to hear something new. I thought that, just maybe, I'd picked up my dad's voice.

Of course, I knew in my head that was impossible. But I think, somewhere in my heart, I was still hoping. Part of me still didn't want to give up. That was why I was never able to get rid of the Skysensor.

I leaned forward and put my ear up to the radio's speaker to hear this new noise. I listened carefully as I made small adjustments to the left and right.

"—rate..."

My ears picked up a sound buried in the white noise that was clearly different. I raised the volume and adjusted the dial at micrometer increments. Well, not literally, of course.

But the feeling I had when I spent the whole day listening to the radio after Dad died came back to me, and I concentrated my whole mind on my ears and fingertips.

"—rate...the world will be..."

This time I could understand it. It was a voice. Words. Japanese. I held my breath to try and understand what it was saying, when... suddenly, the voice stopped.

"That was a girl's voice, wasn't it?" If nothing else, I knew it wasn't my dad, which was a little disappointing.

But that meant the radio must have picked up a signal from somewhere. I decided that I wanted to hear the girl's voice again. It felt like she wanted to tell me something.

"I think she was saying something like, 'At this rate, the world will be...'" Maybe I'd picked up a radio drama that was being broadcast from some station somewhere.

But that was impossible. I'd had the Skysensor set to only pick up shortwave signals. And these days, nobody was broadcasting radio dramas via shortwave.

"Maybe Dad would've known what it was." I knelt down over the Skysensor again.

After that, I tried fiddling with the dials, and even turning it off and back on again, but I never heard that voice a second time. The next thing I knew I was soaked with sweat from the heat, and very thirsty.

I leaned back against the bench, exhausted, and looked up at the twilight summer sky. The sun was setting behind the ten-story condo building in front of me. It felt really bright. I put my hand up to block it out.

At that moment, the world was divided into the colors of twilight, and the black of elongated shadows. Thanks to the condo building in front of me, the whole park was inside the shadow.

The shadows seemed somehow especially black. I don't know why it seemed that way to me. Normally, you never think about how dark a shadow is.

Suddenly something moved in the corner of my vision. It was in the center of the park, on top of a colorful piece of playground equipment.

I looked over, not sure what I was expecting to find... Just in time to see her "land" on top of the slide.

How long had she been there?

I could see the whole park from where I was sitting. If you wanted to get from the entrance to the slide in the center of the park, you needed to walk at least five meters. When did she enter the park? When did she get up on the playground equipment? When did she jump onto the slide? I couldn't figure it out.

And then her voluptuous body began to slip. She slid down the slide like a surfer, and pitched forward at the bottom. She almost fell on her face, but managed to spread out her arms to keep her balance on one foot. Then, staggering from left to right, she made her way over to the bench I was sitting on.

I was...in love. It was hard to believe she was human. I really thought that she was an angel from heaven.

That's why I couldn't move. I just sat on the bench like an idiot, watching as she lurched toward me.

Just when I flinched, ready for a collision, she finally stopped right in front of my face. "Ponya!" She shouted a word I didn't understand, before stretching upwards and raising her arms out in a Y shape. "Ultra-C!"

Before I saw her face, I saw her massive, amazing breasts wobbling in front of me. "Uwah?!" I lurched back without thinking, and only then did our eyes meet.

She was a girl about my age with big eyes. There was something very strange about the way she was looking at me.

"Good Mornighternoon!" That was the first thing she said to me. It was a little different than what Arale used to say in that old anime.

"G-good mornighternoon..." I wasn't quite sure how to respond.

The next thing I felt was a strong sensation of guilt and shame. My face went red from embarrassment, since I'd been staring at her giant breasts when she was so close. But if I moved even a little, I'd touch them, so I couldn't even run.

"I-shi-shu! Hands to the sky, pardner!" Then suddenly, something was pointing at the side of my head. Out of the corner of my eye, I could just barely make out a silver... was that a handgun?

Had she been she holding that a second ago? I couldn't tell. I hadn't noticed it at all. And since I couldn't move, I couldn't even tell if the gun was real or not.

"Hands up, or I'll shoot! ☆" I was even more confused by the lack of tension in her voice. I slowly raised my hands up, being careful not to touch her breasts.

"What is your name, milord?"

"I... I didn't look at your boobs! So please don't kill me..."

"Ididntlook Atyourboobs?"

"Oh, my name? My name is, uh... Yuta Gamon."

"Gamotan!"

No one had ever called me *that* before.

"Ryotasu's name is Ryotasu!" That was her way of introducing herself, evidently. But I had no idea what she meant. I got even more confused.

"Who are you?" I whispered.

"I-shi-shu! ☆" Suddenly, a shock ran through my whole body.

"Abababababababah!" A rainbow-colored flash of light filled my vision. My whole body spasmed like it was struck with lightning, and it wouldn't move. It felt like I was going crazy. My body felt like it was being poked with pins and needles all over. I realized that Ryotasu had actually shot me.

"Stop it...Agigigigigh!" I realized that at some point my head had become buried in Ryotasu's breasts, and I reacted to this emergency by swiftly pulling away.

Then, the pain suddenly stopped. All the strength left my body, and I collapsed to the ground.

How could she just shoot me like that? This girl was crazy. Even if she was cute, that didn't make it okay.

I looked up, panting, just in time to see Ryotasu wink and bring the gun to her lips. It was a toy ray gun, with a retro design and a ball at the end of the barrel.

Then she put her face right up against mine. And right next to my face, she blew a sharp breath out over the top of the gun. Her breath had a sweet scent, like peaches, that made me feel excited.

Her clear eyes were looking down on me, so close that I could touch them. With the setting sun behind her, they should've been surrounded in shadow, but to me, they looked like they were shining.

They were so beautiful that I felt like I was being drawn inside, and I forgot to breathe. The next thing I knew, the pain and sweating were gone.

As I sat there, trying to remind myself of how her breasts felt before I forgot—

"I am—!" She smiled happily, and gently rubbed my cheek, and this is what she said. "—your servant familiar, Gamotan!"

That was my first meeting with the strange girl named Ryoka Narusawa, also known as Ryotasu.

Ever since then, I saw Ryotasu almost every day. But I still didn't know where she came from, or what exactly her Poyaya Gun was.

The biggest mystery was why she was friends with a NEET God like me, though. She was a very mysterious girl. The kind you'd find in an H-game, honestly. But none of that mattered, as long as she was cute. Ryotasu was my angel.

When I went to the roof of the school to meet my angel, the freezing wind brushed past my cheek. The only place at Seimei High where you could go out onto the roof was the four-story central building where the middle and high school students held class. Choosing the roof for a meeting on a cold day like this was a mistake.

If it were me, I would've used the cold as an excuse to give up and go home. But my mysterious Ryotasu was standing at the edge of the empty roof, pointing her PYG through the chain-link fence and pulling the trigger. I could hear her cries of "I-shi-shu!" being carried on the wind.

"Ryotasu!" There was no answer. She was too busy shooting the PYG. Of course, she was probably just pretending. That thing actually *did* fire beams, so it was probably illegal. I really wished she'd stop shooting me with it.

And—wait, I hadn't brought her up here to randomly shoot her PYG. I sighed and started to walk across the uncovered rooftop.

I stood next to Ryotasu and looked down. I could see the whole of Seimei Academy. There was everything from an elementary school to a university concentrated on the grounds. How big was it, again? I'd heard it was about the size of three Tokyo Domes, I think. Not that I was sure whether that was big or small.

Below us was a row of cherry trees. But, of course, there were no pink flowers. I'd have to wait another month for that. Beneath the trees, the other students were walking home from school.

I could see the sports teams practicing at the big track and baseball stadium near the back. I wasn't sure how they could do that when it was so cold.

I looked to my right and I could see the Seimei University campus. Past that was Kichijoji Station, but the campus buildings blocked my view of it.

"I-shi! ☆" Ryotasu was pulling the trigger of the PYG, which she pointed at the baseball team as they practiced. Did she have it out for the baseball team for some reason? But at this distance, it looked like the stinging effect that always hit me wasn't affecting them.

"Ryotasu? How long are you going to keep doing that?" I could see that Ryotasu's cheeks were turning a little red. She must have been cold, after all. She wasn't even wearing a coat. She was willing to endure the freezing cold, just to keep shooting her PYG.

The wind was tossing her shoulder-length, chestnut-colored hair about. The hem of her skirt was blowing up, and if the wind blew just a little harder, I'd be able to see her panties. Ryotasu didn't seem to

notice at all.

"Hmm. Rare. Extremely rare. Not only is any chance to see Ryotasu in her uniform super-ultra-rare..." I took a glance at her chest. It was bursting forth in a way that none of the other girls' did. "Melons! She's got melons in there! Sweet, ripe melons! Gotta love those boob bags!"

It was really rare for me to see Ryotasu at school. We were in different grades, and I had no idea where she lived. I wasn't a normie, so it was far beyond my capabilities to ask her where she lived. Even when we got together at Café☆Blue Moon for Kirikiri Basara, we mostly just showed up on our own. We never set a time.

Whenever Ryotasu came to Blue Moon, she was always wearing her street clothes. She never wore her uniform. Maybe her house was close, and she went home to change first.

Ryotasu's taste in clothing wasn't what you'd call modern. If you wanted to be nice, you could say it was grown-up. If you didn't, you could say it was old-fashioned.

Either way, it was a little... no, a lot different from what your average teenage girl wore. So when I saw her wearing the same uniform as the other girls, it felt like a nice change of pace. And it reminded me of something very important.

"Every middle and high school in the country should make boob bags mandatory for the girls' uniforms!"

"Gamota~n?" Ryotasu slowly and deliberately turned the PYG toward me.

"You were thinking something naughty, weren't you?"

"Uh..."

"I-shi-shu!" Ryotasu showed no mercy at times like these.

"Ow! Poyaya Gun! No!" I screamed, and Ryotasu stopped.

"Not only were you late, you were thinking naughty things. If you don't hurry, the AV room's gonna escape!"

"Th-the AV room...isn't going to escape. I mean, it's an AV room." I was crawling along the ground and gasping for breath as I spoke.

"I-if there ever were a room that grew legs, I'd want to see it."

"Not the AV room! It's Myu, in the room, that's going to run!"

"Then you should've said that instead."

But Ryotasu was right. There was no guarantee that Myu-Pom would be in the classroom. She might go home while we stood here talking. And so, I slowly staggered to my feet, and went back inside the school with Ryotasu.

The AV room was on the fourth story of the central building. It was right down the stairs from the roof.

"You know, though, I never considered that Myu-Pom might be a student at our school. That was pretty sharp of you, Ryotasu."

"Eh-hem! ☆ I may not look like it, but my nose reaches into all the tiny spots."

"...?"

"Poya? My nose? My nose...hmm...mm..." Ryotasu scratched the tip of her tiny nose for a moment, and then broke into a big smile. "Nose! The nose knows!"

"Yeah, right. Well, anyway, you did great." I'd gone and looked after we'd last talked, and our high school actually had a club called the Fortune-Telling Research Club. They were based out of the central building's AV room. There was a good chance that was where "Myu's Niconico Live Fortune-Telling" was filmed.

The plan was to bust in there and find out if I was right. If I was lucky, I might even get to see Myu-Pom.

"Wow, my heart's going to ker-thud! Ker-heart! My ker-thud's going heart-heart!" I took a bunch of deep breaths as I went down the stairs. Ryotasu didn't even bother waiting for me. She went down the stairs and turned the corner. I followed her into the hallway, and then—

"GAH," I yelled.

There was a crowd of about ten students in front of the AV room.

It wasn't just high school students, too. Some of them were in middle school. I guess that was natural, though, since the middle school and high school students used the same building here. There were five boys and six girls. They didn't seem to know each other, too.

They seemed to be split up into four groups: three middle school girls, two high school boys, another group of three high school boys, and then three high school girls. All of them were whispering in low voices as they tried to see what was going on in the AV room.

What were they all doing here? Were they all part of the fortune-telling club? But then why didn't they go inside? Or was this just the line for people to have their fortunes told by Myu-Pom?

The door to the AV room was closed. If the stream had already started, I was too late.

"Oh, there she is! She's so cute! Come on, Samurai Gamonosuke! Get over here! ☆" Ryotasu was clinging to the door of the AV room and shouting excitedly.

Grrh... That's not fair, Ryotasu! It's not fair that you didn't wait for me! And I'm not a samurai, too!

I could feel the other students staring at me, but I followed Ryotasu's lead and looked through the window on the door into the AV room.

"Nnnuuhhh! That's definitely our idol, Myu Aikawa!" I had been sure that she was live, but she wasn't.

The curtain to the AV room was still open. Inside, four girls were sitting around the table, having what looked like a meeting. There were snacks and candy on the table, and three of the four girls had relaxed expression on their faces. It felt like a bunch of high school girls having a chat. But one of the four girls was looking glum as she stared down at the cards in her hand.

That was Myu Aikawa. The last two times she'd been on "Myu's Niconico Livestream," she'd broken down in tears. Maybe that's why she wasn't looking so good. I was a little worried about her, but more importantly...

"Ryotasu! She's really there! Wow! It's really her! Tens of thousands of people have seen her streaming from here, huh?" It was clear now that Myu Aikawa was a student at our school.

What was her real name? What grade was she in? And wait, how had I been at this school for two years without noticing a perfectly pretty girl like her?

I guess I couldn't help it. I couldn't even remember the names of my classmates. I was the NEET God, after all. I bet the rest of the school was already talking about her all the time. I hated myself for being such a wrong-sider.

Myu-Pom showed no signs of noticing us on the other side of the door. The other girls looked worried as they talked to her. She let her frown drop and tried her best to smile.

Yeah. She was such a nice girl. She was trying her best not to let the other members of the club worry about her.

I'm in love. Marry me, please.

Anyway, were they going to stream more of "Myu's Niconico Live Fortune-Telling" today? There never seemed to be any rule about what day it aired, but it always began at about 6:00 PM and lasted a little under an hour. That was probably because the school closed around then. But that meant that if I wanted to talk to Myu-Pom, I'd need to wait here until about after 7:00 PM.

Now that I knew Myu Aikawa was a student at my school, I'd achieved my immediate goal, but, if I was going to be writing more about her on Kirikiri Basara, I wanted a little more of her private information. And if I could, I wanted to get an interview with her.

And maybe, if I could, I'd want to be her friend, too. Maybe. Possibly.

No, no, no! No way! No way! No way! How was I supposed to introduce myself to her?

"I'm a fan of yours. Please shake my hand."

Wait, that would just make me look like a groupie.

"I've come to wipe away your tears."

Yeah, that's enough to make any girl fall in love! But only if the speaker is hot. In other words, I'd make that backfire completely.

"Milady, I am a millionaire who makes big bucks off my anti-occult affiliate blog, Kirikiri Basara!"

Wait, that's the worst thing I could say! I'm supposed to be talking to Myu-Pom, the fortune-teller from TV and magazines! Fortune-telling is part of the occult! If I told Myu-Pom I ran an anti-occult blog...

She'd hate me for sure! Okay, no telling her about Kirikiri Basara. Sounds good. That's the safest route. First impressions are important.

But that would make it hard to write about Myu-Pom on Kirikiri Basara. I couldn't run an interview without her permission.

Uwaaah! What am I supposed to do?!

"Ahem. Young samurai. Are you not going inside?"

"Huh?" I snapped back to my senses just as Ryotasu was about to open the door.

"Uwah! Time out! Time out!" I managed to grab her hand just in time.

"Po-yah-yah?"

"You can't just walk in there."

"But they're just chatting, it seems like."

"Yeah, but..."

"You came to talk to her, right?"

"Ugh... I'm not sure what to do about that." I still wasn't sure if I should tell her who I was or not. For now, I needed to make a strategic retreat.

And then, I felt someone behind me, staring at me. I turned around, not really expecting to see much of anything.

"Uh..." Ten pairs of angry eyes were staring at me and Ryotasu. All the other students in the hallway had surrounded me from a distance and were glaring at me. There was real hate in their eyes.

Did I do something wrong? I could hear whispers.

"Who are they?"

"If they're planning to cut in line, we crush them."

"These assholes probably don't even know what they're doing."

"They're not even saying a word to our Aikawa fan club, huh?"

I heard the voices, and finally understood who they were. They were all Myu-Pom fans! I hadn't even considered that she might have fans in the school besides me. It was completely unexpected.

And I'd just walked right up to the door and ignored them.

They'd decided that I was an enemy and interloper. If this were an idol concert, I would've been in big trouble. If Ryotasu and I tried to talk to Myu-Pom when she left the AV room, they'd interrupt me somehow for sure. At least, that's what I would've done in their place.

M-maybe I should just suck up to them and see if they'd let me join their club. But now that they'd already made their first impressions of me, it was impossible to imagine that working. And I didn't have the communications skills necessary to bring them around to my side.

Grrh... I should've been more careful. But who the hell would've thought she'd have fans waiting for her to leave her room? She wasn't an idol singer or anything. Did they think that since Myu-Pom was an amateur, she'd be more than happy to talk to them? Or were they like those guys who thought that they were cool because they were supporting an unknown singer?

I could understand the girls wanting to get closer to the fortune-teller everyone was talking about online, but while yuri in anime and manga was one thing, yuri in real life was just creepy. *Go chase after some boy idols or something, girls.*

"Gamonosuke? What are you mumbling about?"

Oh crap. Was I saying this stuff out loud? Ryotasu and I continued our conversation in a whisper.

"These people are all just jumping on the latest trend. I wish they wouldn't get in our way."

"You are too, Gamotan!"

"Wait, I'm doing what, too?"

"Jumping, jumping on the latest trend! ♪ " Ryotasu pointed at me and suddenly started to sing in a louder volume. She spun her finger in a circle as she hummed a short melody.

"I'm...just following a trend, too?" I stood there in shock for a moment, and then looked at the other fans again.

The three girls from middle school were glaring at me particularly hard.

"Who's that creepy kid? Is he a fan of Aikawa? What's he doing, bringing another girl here?"

"What a jerk. I wish he'd just die."

"If he tries to go after our Aikawa, we kill him."

I can hear every word you're saying! I'd love to hear those words from a middle school girl in an anime or something, but hearing them in real life was really depressing! Anyway, it was best to just not look at them.

All I wanted to do for today was stand in the corner and get a look at Myu-Pom from a distance. So I yanked Ryotasu away from the door and headed for the back of the line. And then the fans started to mutter and fidget.

Maybe the fortune-telling club was done with its meeting? When I'd looked inside a moment ago, it had seemed like they were mostly chatting.

I looked at the clock. It was still before 5:00 PM. Myu-Pom's livestream was always held at 6:00 PM or so, so that would mean there was over an hour or two to go.

"Is she coming? Is she coming?"

The door to the AV room opened, and Myu-Pom came out.

"Wow, it's really her!" I leaned forward and shouted, despite myself. And then—

Our eyes met.

She looked just like she did on the livestream. No, her face might actually have been a little smaller, even.

The famous, just-right beauty, the fortune-teller that everyone loved, Myu Aikawa, was right there. And for some reason, she was looking at me, a NEET who ran an affiliate blog. Her eyes were open wide with surprise, and her lips were trembling a little.

"You're—"

"Huh?"

And then the other fans surrounded Myu-Pom, and I lost sight of her.

Grr... They were seriously in the way! Not only had they treated me like an interloper, they wouldn't even let me look at her from a distance! What a bunch of jerks. I cursed at them in my mind, but my heart was beating faster.

Myu-Pom was staring at me. She seemed surprised. It looked like she was trying to say something to me. What was she saying? Was I imagining it?

"Hey, hey, Gamonosuke. You sure you don't want to do an interview?"

"N-no. That's impossible. If I tried to talk to her like this, it would just be weird. I'm not the kind of normie who could just go up to a girl I'd never met and talk to her, anyway. The only reason I came here today was to see if Myu-Pom was a student at my school, and I didn't actually plan on interviewing her. And anyway, if I wanted an interview, I'd just send you, Ryotasu. I'd just appointed you 'Correspondent' a little bit ago. She won't be as nervous talking to you as she would be talking to a guy."

"Gamotan." Ryotasu put her hand on my shoulder, smiling. "You're a pretty wimpy samurai today, huh, Gamonosuke?"

"Grr... Hearing that from a girl with a big grin on her face is really depressing."

Anyway, those fans were getting right up in Myu-Pom's face. Could she even move with all of them that close? And what did they want from her, anyway? A handshake? An autograph? A photo? Or did they want her to tell their fortunes?

"Stop blocking her! You're bothering Miyuu!" The other members of the fortune-telling club were trying their best to push through the wall of fans, but it wasn't working.

At this rate, it would take a half hour for them to deal with all the fans. There was no point in waiting here. I should just go home. It was enough just to know that she was here.

Just when I was about to tell Ryotasu we were leaving—

"Let me through!" A sharp voice rose up through the crowd. The whole place went silent.

"I'm sorry. I'm really sorry. Just let me through, please." The crowd parted to let Myu-Pom through.

Myu-Pom came walking up to me, unsteadily. She took a breath, and looked up, straight into my eyes. She looked sad, almost like she was about to cry.

"Huh? Huh?" Me? Why was she looking at me? She'd been doing that before, too. Did I know her? Maybe I'd forgotten it, but we used to play together a decade ago? Did things like that ever happen to me? No, they didn't. I was sure of it.

Then why? Myu-Pom took a step forward, and then another. I was frozen in place. I wanted to run, but I couldn't.

At last, she stood in front of me and froze in place.

She smelled really good. Her soft white hand reached out and

grabbed mine.

I heard what sounded like muffled gasps of shock coming from her fans. But Myu-Pom ignored them, and held my hand as she whispered.

"I've been waiting for you."

▶ site 18: Aria Kurenaino ——————— 2/19 (Friday)

My house was a thirty-minute walk from Kichijoji Station. I always closed my black magic agency, the House of Crimson in Harmonica Alley, late at night. Typically, well past midnight.

Since it was within walking distance, I never worried about catching the last train. Actually, I looked forward to walking home through the quiet, chill air. Especially at this time of year, everything was so quiet that it was like the world itself was frozen.

The darkness was a gentle veil that could hide a tiny girl like me from sight. Inside the dark, I felt more peace than fear.

I especially felt this way when I passed by Zenpukuji Park, which was right next to my house. If the darkness were to come all the way up to my feet, I would gladly offer myself up to it.

I made it back to my house just in time to see Mr. Mishima, who lived across the way, come back home. His luxury car quietly parked in its spot. He emerged from the car, a middle-aged gentleman who I'd heard worked at a bank or something similar.

Since our eyes met, I gave him a small greeting, but he regarded me the same way you might a pile of garbage before he headed inside.

I was used to people acting that way. If you asked my neighbors, my house and I were something to be avoided, and something that would hopefully go away altogether someday.

Even in a wealthy area like this, my home was a mansion bigger than the others. But it only looked impressive on the outside. Since I lived alone, I wasn't able to keep it up, and in places, it was starting to show.

Every time there was a big earthquake, I was worried that this time, the whole place would just collapse. That wouldn't be the worst way to go, of course.

In fall, nuts would fall off of the gingko trees and generate a horrible smell. I didn't like the smell, but I accepted it as just part of the way things were.

When I opened the front door, the squeak sounded like an old woman's scream. Of course, inside, it was dark, and there was no sign of life.

I coughed a little when I entered. It was always dusty, but I had no intention of cleaning it up. If I did, the dark stagnation that swirled around this house would disappear. I would entrust myself to the stagnation, even when it was so thick I wanted to vomit.

That was what a black magic agent like me deserved.

I walked up the stairs to my room without even bothering to turn on the lights. "I'm home," I spoke into the room.

Until two years ago, I would've always heard a voice saying, "Welcome back."

Instead, I was met with row after row of silent dolls. I probably had over a hundred of them now. Even I, their creator, had forgotten their exact number. I'd just stopped counting.

I took off my coat and threw it aside, and then fell face-first into a rococo-style bed with a magnificent canopy. Lately, whenever I came home, I would fall straight into bed without taking a bath or even eating first.

I never woke up early. I would usually sleep until noon. Since I was lucky to get two customers a day at my black magic agency, I wasn't exactly busy, either.

I liked to think that I was living the life I wanted, but maybe it was wearing me down and I just hadn't realized it yet.

"Brother..." I whispered, with my eyes closed. It felt like if I did, I would hear my beloved brother answer me.

You'll catch cold if you sleep like that, Ria.

I missed him. But the man I loved was gone now.

Until just two years ago, my brother had been the only color in my life. I remembered those days, and how happy I was.

My parents had died when I was only ten years old. Ever since then, I'd lived alone with my brother in this huge mansion.

He was tall, and a good athlete, and he even said someone had scouted him as a model once. He got the best grades in his class, and he'd graduated K University as valedictorian. He was the person I admired more than anyone else in the world.

He was thirteen years older than me, and I had no way of knowing how much he'd sacrificed to raise me when I was young. I had just been happy to be with my brother, the only family I had in the world.

I was always introverted, and I wasn't really good at talking to people. Brother told me that I should go to school, so I did, but honestly, I would've rather spent every hour of the day at home with him.

Brother had to work. Our parents had left us a lot of money, but Brother didn't think it was right to just live off of that instead of working. So he wasn't able to spend all his time with me.

For the first few years, he often left for work early in the morning. He still managed to make it in time for dinner, but I was so lonely in this big mansion while I waited for him to come home.

Everything at school was terrible, too. My classmates were mean to me, and my teacher looked at me with creepy eyes and sometimes touched me.

I knew my gentle brother was tired from work, but he still listened to all of my problems. I wanted to be alone with him, forever.

"I don't want to go anywhere else. I don't want you to go anywhere else. Brother, don't go to work. If you go, I'll bite off my own tongue and kill myself..."

"I feel the same way as you, Ria. I want to live with you quietly here, forever. But if we want to survive, I have to work. I'm sorry, Ria." When I told him my selfish, crazy request, he just smiled like he wasn't sure what to do.

That all suddenly changed around the time when I turned fourteen. One day, I started to hyperventilate on the way to school, and they took me to the hospital. After that, my brother quit his job and started to spend the whole day with me.

He would wait patiently for me to come home from school. He listened with deep interest, and not the slightest sign of revulsion, to me telling him about the things that I'd just learned about black magic. Morning and night, he'd smile and tell me the food I made was delicious.

When I went to bed, he would snuggle up next to me. He would gently rub my head as I lay on my pillow, and say, "Goodnight, Ria. Sweet dreams. I hope you have a wonderful tomorrow."

My favorite thing in the morning was to get up earlier than he did, and then wake him up.

That year was the happiest in my life. My wish ever since I was a child—to be with my brother forever—had come true. No matter what awful things happened outside, when I got home, my brother would be waiting for me in my room. No matter how much my classmates, the male teachers, or the strange men on the streets looked at me with dirty eyes, I was able to endure it.

"You're a very charming girl, Ria, so perhaps those men can't help but fall prey to your charms. I wish I could protect you, but I can't really go with you to school."

"It's all right, Brother. As long as you're here to hold me in your arms, I can endure anything."

"You're such a good girl, Ria. But if you really can't handle something, tell me, okay? I'll do whatever it takes to get revenge for you. And I'll never let them get near you again."

"Thank you, Brother. I love you."

Only when Brother held me in his arms could I forget about the outside world.

But that happiness didn't last long. It happened on a cold day, like this one. I had only a week or so to go before I graduated middle school.

When I came back from school that day, my quiet house was filled with noise. There were lots of cars parked in front of the yard. Some of them were patrol cars and ambulances.

It was winter, but the house was filled with a terrible stench, probably from the gingko nuts in the yard. Confused, I went inside just in time to see my brother being carried out on a stretcher.

"Who are you people? What are you doing to my brother?! Don't touch my brother!"

He was asleep, as if he'd been injected with some kind of drug, and he didn't answer to my voice. The stretcher was surrounded by police officers and EMTs, and other people I didn't know. They wouldn't let me get close.

"You can't just take my brother from me! This is kidnapping! I'll call the police right now!"

"Ria! Calm down!"

"How can I calm down? You're taking away the only family I've got left! Brother! Wake up! Brother! Brother!"

I grabbed onto the stretcher, knocking it over. My brother's body fell to the floor. He didn't move, but the other adults around me began to panic.

"Someone! Grab Ria!"

"Don't take my brother away! Don't steal him from me!" I leapt on top of my brother's body as if to protect him.

But they grabbed me from behind and pulled me away. A fifteen-year-old girl wasn't strong enough to resist multiple grown-ups.

"No! Let me go! Brother! Help me! Brother!"

"Stop fighting! How long do you plan to keep acting like this! It's... It's not normal!"

"Not normal?" When I heard those words, for the first time, I took a good look at the adults around me. "What do you mean?"

They were looking at me with revulsion and fear. That wasn't how you were supposed to look at a fifteen-year-old girl. It wasn't how you were supposed to look at a human being.

I'd felt this way before. My classmates, the male teachers, the men I passed on the street... They'd all looked at me, at my body, with filthy eyes.

I felt the same shiver down my spine as they looked at me now. The tears wouldn't stop coming. I couldn't let them do this. I couldn't let them say that my relationship with my brother wasn't normal.

No matter how hard I tried to grit my teeth, the tears wouldn't stop, and I felt a rage about to explode in the depths of my heart.

"You all think that I've seduced my brother into committing incest, don't you? You adults, with your disgusting prejudices against black magic, are far worse than I am! It's true that I love my brother. But we've never had the sort of tainted relationship you're thinking about. Is it wrong for a pair of siblings to simply love one another?"

"That's not even close to being the problem here, Ria!" I recognized the pale, middle-aged woman who was grabbing me by the shoulders and shaking me. She was my mother's younger sister. My aunt.

"But then what..."

"Can't you see what's really happening?"

"Really...happening?"

"The neighbors called the cops because of the smell!"

"The smell?" The house was still full of a smell like rotten eggs. I'd thought it was strange that we had gingko nuts in winter, but I'd gotten so used to the smell that I didn't really think about it anymore.

"What are you talking about? What..."

"Listen carefully, Ria." My aunt's voice was shaking. "Your brother died *a year ago!*"

"What?" I didn't understand what she was saying. "He died? But that's impossible. I mean, he's right..."

I looked down at my brother, lying on the floor. But in an instant, my brother—the tall boy, the athletic boy, the boy who'd once been scouted as a model—had transformed into a dried-up mummy.

"Myu Aikawa, the famous teenage fortune-telling girl, has joined the staff of Kirikiri Basara!" I was in a state of huge excitement after this miraculous occurrence yesterday, and of course, I was in the mood to brag about it on Twitter. It was like a dream come true.

I mean, can you believe it? That means I've got two hot girls, Ryotasu and Myu-Pom, working for a niche blog like Kirikiri Basara. No doubt about it: this made me a normie.

But when I woke up this morning, the excitement of the moment had faded, and I was starting to have second thoughts. And, as a result, I lost the chance to announce the big news, which could've been a huge boost to my traffic numbers.

It wasn't "like a dream come true." It was a dream. I had to be dreaming. And if I wasn't dreaming, something was up. At least, that's how it felt to me.

"Hello, excuse me." Café ☆ Blue Moon still wasn't open.

I led Myu-Pom—she'd told me yesterday that her real name was Miyuu Aikawa—inside the café. She looked a little surprised at the decorations.

"Yahhh! Wow, it's the real Myu!" Master Izumin shouted in his creepy way and leapt out from behind the counter. He pushed me aside and grabbed Myu by the hand.

"Can I shake your hand?!" It seemed like a waste of time to point out that he already was.

Master Izumin kept a firm grip on Myu-Pom's hand as the two exchanged introductions.

"I always read your fortune-telling articles."

"Really? That makes me super happy."

"Hey, Gamota! Gamota! Can you take a picture? A picture of me and Myu! It's okay, right, Myu?"

"Oh, sure. That's fine. Ahaha..." Myu-Pom looked a little overwhelmed, and couldn't bring herself to refuse. I saw no choice but to take the photo he wanted.

"Aw, that's so great! I want a photo with Myu, too!"

Come on, Ryotasu. At least pretend to have some social grace... Eh, I guess that's impossible.

I was starting to get a stomachache. Since Myu-Pom was working for Kirikiri Basara, I'd brought her here to our base of operations.

But I still wasn't 100% sure how or why she'd ended up working with us. And I still hadn't told her the most important thing, that Kirikiri Basara was an anti-occult blog. That was one of the reasons I'd brought her here. But how to tell her?

"Oh, my phone's ringing. Excuse me." Myu-Pom took her phone out of her bag. It was vibrating.

"Oh, Chi? I'm fine. I told you a bunch of times already, I'm just fine. You're too worried. They haven't done anything weird to me.

Really."

What did she mean by "weird"? I had no choice but to stand there and wait for her to finish her call. Which meant, of course, that I heard everything she was saying. But I couldn't help it, right?

"Yeah, thanks, Chi. Yeah. See you tomorrow. Bye-bye." Myu-Pom hung up with a smile and bowed. "Sorry to keep you waiting."

"Was that a friend?"

"Oh, right. She's from my fortune-telling club. She's a super nice girl. She's always worried about me. Want me to introduce you to her?"

"N-no! No way!"

Crap! That sounded really weird!

"Huh? 'No way'? You think you're too good for her? Well, I'm not letting you have her, anyway!" Myu-Pom sounded a little upset, but she quickly broke into a grin. She seemed to understand that I didn't mean anything by it.

Myu-Pom spun around and looked at the café, seemingly impressed. "This is a really cute café, huh?"

C-cute? TIL that I had no idea what Myu thought was cute.

"Thank you! You're welcome any time, Myu. Any time at all!"

Master Izumin kept interrupting. *I let you get a photo, so back off, you pervert master.*

"Did you choose this café because you liked the decorations, Gamon?"

"Huh? Oh, yeah..."

"Hmm... I like it. It works. But it doesn't really feel like your kind of thing." For some reason, she seemed to be looking me over from head to toe.

Yeah, that was a compliment. *There's such a thing as gap moe, right*? She must have felt some kind of potential within me that was unimaginable from my boring appearance, and been struck by my gap moe! *Uwaaaah! Now I'm feeling excited! Well done, Blue Moon!*

"Wouldn't this be a great place to do my fortune-telling livestream? It's got more atmosphere than the place we do it now."

"Oh my, you mean your Niconico Livestream? I'd love that! I bet the customers would, too!"

Master Izumin, shut up!

"So, Gamon, is this where you do your work for Kirikiri Saraba?"

"Oh... It's Basara, not Saraba."

"Umyu? I see. If it was Saraba, you'd be cutting goodbyes, right?"

"Th-that's right. Well, for an occult blog, maybe Saraba would be a better name...maybe."

"Sorry. I got it wrong."

"Nah, I'm sorry."

The two of us bowed to each other.

"You two get along, huh?" Ryotasu laughed.

So did Myu-Pom. I grinned. This was turning into a romantic comedy. Is this how it felt to be a normie? If so, then I loved it! It was a little embarrassing, and really wonderful! My heart wouldn't stop pounding! *Marry me!*

"Oh, sit down. Um, what will you have to drink? Oh, but don't get your hopes up. The owner's so stingy, he won't give you anything but water, eheheh..."

"Excuse me, Gamota? I'm sorry to interrupt you when you're getting your creepy laugh on, but if you're willing to pay, I'll bring you soft drinks. Don't get the wrong idea, okay?"

"Tsundere Master for the win! Bring us three waters!"

"Bring them yourself." He got me the glasses, ice, and nothing else.

Since I had no other choice, I brought the waters from the counter to the table, and placed one in front of Myu-Pom.

"Thank you. You're really nice, Gamon."

R-really nice?! All you had to do to be "really nice" was bring her water?! I'd never been told that by a girl my age! Now I was *really* excited!

"Wait, hold it! I know what 'nice' means. Nice means 'total beta who would never put the moves on a girl,' doesn't it? I know it does."

"No, I didn't say that..."

"No, I mean, you're absolutely right, ma'am!"

"Wait, why are you calling me 'ma'am' when you're older than me?"

"Oh, um... well..."

"You can just talk your usual way."

"O-okay...roger that, milady."

"Oh! It's Samurai Gamonosuke!" Ryotasu started to clap.

Myu-Pom was watching her with a grin.

"Are you blushing, Gamon?"

"I am."

"Ahaha, that's hilarious. Even though I'm younger than you?"

"I'm blushing."

"Gamonosuke is a blushing pervert samurai, after all."

"Ryotasu? Who are you calling a pervert?" Myu-Pom stared at me, then Ryotasu, then back at me again.

"Wh-what is it?"

"Are you and Narusawa... Oh, wait, Narusawa's a first-year student, isn't she?"

"That's right. I'm a fresh young freshman!"

"Are you two dating?"

"*Cough* *hack*"

"I mean, when you two came to the fortune-telling club yesterday, you were together. And the two of you have been running Kirikiri Saraba together this whole time, right?"

"Um... it's not Saraba..."

"Oh, right. Right. So, are you dating?"

"Ryotasu is Gamotan's servant familiar! ☆ Sparkle-ting! ☆"

"Is that, um... some kind of code word for something naughty? Is that the kind of guy you are, Gamon? If that's the case, then that's super-creepy."

"Th-that servant familiar thing is just something Ryotasu says! I'm just the admin of Kirikiri Basara and she's my correspondent. That's all!" Of course, I would've been happy to get involved in "something naughty" with Ryotasu. But I was the NEET God, and didn't have the courage to ask a real girl out. Not even close.

"But Gamotan's had me threaten him with a ray gun before!"

"What?! Gamon, you threatened her with a gun?! She'll turn you over to the police! I thought you were a nice person, but maybe I was wrong!"

"No, you need to listen more carefully. She was the one who threatened me."

"Huh? She threatened you?"

"Yeah. The first time we met. And actually, she shot me."

Myu-Pom looked over at Ryotasu to see if I was telling the truth. Ryotasu nodded, grinning.

"It's true, then... You two have a really special relationship, don't you? I won't ask for more details, then."

She was looking at me like I was a pervert! Man, this was embarrassing. It was like somebody found out about my fetishes. I could feel my face turn as red as a boiled octopus. I took a gulp of cold water to hide it.

"Listen, why are you asking me so many questions? Do you *cough* like me, or something? *Cough* If you do, I'm just fine with choosing you instead of her."

"Are you okay?"

"Oh, sorry... the water went down the wrong pipe."

"Narusawa, is Gamon always like this?"

"I think he's just a little excited. Right, Gamotan?"

"Are you excited, Gamon?"

"I am, I sure am! This is like a dream come true! I've never played an H-game, but I bet this is what they're like! I'm half-convinced it's some big conspiracy! Right now, I'm literally wondering if your friend Chi isn't hiding in the shadows and recording all this so that you can upload it to Nico and make fun of me!"

"Chi wouldn't do that."

"Then why are you getting my hopes up like this?! Why did you come with me to this creepy-ass bar?! When did I turn into a normie?! This whole thing is impossible! If this is a dream, I want to wake up! No, actually, I don't!"

"Excuse me, Gamota? What do you mean, 'creepy-ass bar'? If you're going to be a brat, I'll kick you out."

"*Cough* That's not what I meant, Master Izumin."

"Gamon, you're being kinda creepy." I could see the smile frozen on Myu-Pom's face.

She said I was creepy. I guess I got too excited. Damn it. It was time to calm down. I didn't want her hating me even more.

Ryotasu brought me another glass of water, and I gulped it down. Whew...

I sat back in my chair and took several deep breaths, secretly glancing at Myu-Pom to see how she was doing. The popular female fortune-teller was having a nice chat with Ryotasu.

"Myu, have you ever had the frozen yogurt from Woodberrys?"

"Oh, I have!"

"Wow! How was it? How was it?"

"It was super-good! It's crazy!"

"I'm so jealous..."

"Do you like it?"

"Poya... I've never been. Poyan..."

"Then let's go sometime!"

"No, I can't. Gamotan told me he'd take me. I'm still waiting for him."

Sh-she remembered?

"Are you two sure you aren't dating?"

"Pohya-yah?"

Okay...I'd finally calmed down, and I was ready to ask her the question I'd been wondering this whole time.

"Um, Myu-Pom... er, Aikawa. Yesterday, when you said you'd been waiting for me. What did that mean?"

Myu-Pom suddenly sat up straight. It felt like she'd been waiting for me to ask that question.

"My fortune-telling told me that if I were with you, it would open up a path to my future."

"Huh?"

"That's the reason. It's kind of selfish. I'm sorry." She bowed deeply, but...

"You told your own fortune?"

"Yes."

"What happens if you're with me?"

"I don't know."

"Um... you know the blog I run, right? Kirikiri Basara? It's anti-occult, and it's what's called an affiliate blog, which means I make money by..."

"I know the basics, yeah. I know what it says, and I know what everybody says about it. I looked it up yesterday after I got home."

"Oh, I see." She already knew, huh?

"Th-then you know what that means, right? I'm a scummy NEET who's going to use your fortune-telling to make money."

"I don't care if you're a scummy NEET." Myu-Pom's voice was clear.

So she's not denying that I'm a scummy NEET, huh?

"I've still decided that I'm better off together with you."

Uwah... I could feel a kind of incredible resolve coming from within her, and it gave me goosebumps. I could tell that the results of her fortune-telling were really important to her. It made sense, since she was a fortune-teller, after all. For a guy like me, who didn't believe in the occult, her earnestness made me a little jealous in a way I didn't understand.

"Is that not good enough?"

Either way, when she stared at me with those needy eyes, how could I not blush? I looked away.

Um... I needed to say something. I needed to say something cool.

"B-by the way, if you do join Kirikiri Basara's staff, I want to do a bunch of interviews, and maybe have you do articles for the site, and maybe some events, like handshake events, and then maybe you and Ryotasu can go out and be correspondents and find us stuff to report on. That'll mean that Kirikiri Basara is sure to be a super-famous affiliate blog! We'll get tons of affiliate cash, and I won't have to work!"

"Y-you're planning to make me do all that?"

Oh no! I panicked! I'm doomed! If I keep talking like this, Myu-Pom is going to knock over her chair and run out of the room! I need to get back on track! "U-um, but Kirikiri Basara is going to promote you heavily. So it's a win-win, right?"

"Win-Win Don-Dorurururu! Grandpa's DOHC!" Ryotasu started making noises like a car engine, but I ignored her.

Myu-Pom didn't look especially mad when she heard me. "I don't really need you to promote me, but if you'll hire me, I'll do what I can."

"So maybe a swimsuit photo shoot..."

"Not happening."

"Haha, yeah... didn't think so." Still, she really wanted to be with me, huh? It felt like I was the only person who had anything to gain here, but if Myu-Pom was okay with this, then there was nothing more for me to say. Otherwise, she might change her mind.

"Then it's settled. I look forward to working with you, Myu-Pom."

"Huh? Myu...Pom?"

Oh, crap...

"Th-the staff at Kirikiri Basara all use nicknames for each other! Your nickname is Myu-Pom! That's my decision and I'm sticking to it! Ryotasu is Ryotasu!"

"And Gamotan's Gamotan! ☆"

Thank you, Ryotasu!

"So you can call me by a nickname too, if you want. Yuta, maybe?"

"Hmm... I'll go with Gamo."

"That's very...normal."

"Yuta isn't even a nickname, for one thing."

"Haha... yeah. It's not."

"Anyway, I look forward to working with you too, Gamo." Myu-Pom chuckled and bowed to me.

And in that instant, I truly became one of life's winners. From now on, I would be updating my blog after school in the company of two cute younger girls. Talk about being a NEET God! All other NEETs around the world were sure to be jealous of me now.

"I didn't know you could tell your own fortune, though. Didn't Sarai say something about that during your livestream? I think he said that people who couldn't tell their own fortunes were frauds, right?"

"That's right. That ticked me off, so I tried telling my own future."

"Well, Sarai got his butt kicked, and he deserved it, too."

"Do you know him?"

"He's a regular at Kirikiri Basara. I've never met him, though. He was all set to humiliate you, and then he got wrecked. I laughed when I watched it."

Ryotasu's expression suddenly darkened. Was she maybe worried about Sarai? I thought I remembered her saying something about his dad.

"I feel bad for poor Sarai."

"Again, Ryotasu? That's the third time you've said that. I'm sick of hearing it."

"Poyayah..."

Just as Ryotasu looked down, depressed, I suddenly heard a

muffled voice from down by my feet. A cold chill ran down my back. I imagined that someone was underneath my chair, and almost leapt back in fright.

It was a very faint voice. But it started to get louder, and it quickly became clear that I wasn't hallucinating it. It sounded like an angry woman, moaning, her voice coming from deep beneath the Earth.

And suddenly there was a different woman's voice. It wasn't Japanese, but there was a melody, and it sounded like a song. Her voice was sad and lonely. I wondered where it was coming from, but I could only think of one place.

It was the case I always carried on my shoulder. The Skysensor was sitting at my feet right now. The song was coming from the radio's speaker.

The voice was loud enough now that it was filling the whole café. The volume knob must have been turned all the way up, because the clipping was awful. I quickly opened the case and turned down the volume.

"What song is that?"

I glanced at Ryotasu and Myu-Pom, But neither of them seemed to know. I'd never heard the song, either.

It was dark and gloomy, and just hearing it was enough to make me feel down. The audio quality was terrible, so I guessed that it was an old song that wasn't Japanese. I glanced over to the counter and saw that Master Izumin was staring at my radio, looking deathly pale.

"Master Izumin, do you know what song this is?"

"..."

"Master?"

"Huh? O-oh... This song? Of course I know it. It's a really bad one,

I think."

"A bad one? What do you mean?"

In answer to Myu-Pom's question, Master Izumin came out from behind the counter and dropped his voice to a whisper.

"The song's title is, um... something 'Sunday.' What was it, again? 'Lonely'... no...it's not 'Scary,' either... That's right. 'Gloomy Sunday'!"

"Sunday's gloomy? If you ask me, I think Monday's gloomier. ☆"

"Ryotasu, you see, this is something really scary." Master Izumin normally always joked around, but now he was very serious. I started to feel a little scared, too.

"'Gloomy Sunday'... I think I've heard of it, too," Myu-Pom said, but she still didn't seem to fully recall it.

I... I'd never heard of a song like that. "So what's up with this song? Does it have a bad reputation or something?"

"This was an urban legend back when I was in high school, but... hmm... I don't really want to talk about it. It's not exactly pleasant."

"Come on, just tell us! Urban legends are always fake, anyway." Master Izumin sighed and shook his head.

"'Gloomy Sunday' was written about eighty years ago, in Hungary. It's an old song. And the urban legend is that this song...is called the 'Suicide Song.'"

"The 'Suicide Song'?" That sounded like something I could use for Kirikiri Basara.

"Tell me more!"

"The lyrics are about a girl remembering her dead lover. But in the end, she decides to kill herself."

"Is that all? That's not the only reason they call it the 'Suicide Song,' right?" There had to be something more sensational involved if an eighty-year-old song had earned urban legend status.

"There's more to it than that. Here's where it gets serious." He paused for a moment to look around the café . Of course, there was nobody here but the four of us.

"It's said that several hundred people around the world have listened to this song and then actually killed themselves."

Several hundred...

If it had really negative lyrics, maybe someone who already wanted to commit suicide could hear it and then decide to do it? Was that possible?

"I don't feel like dying right now, so I'm fine. ☆ What about you, Myu?"

"I think I'm fine too, but..."

"It's not like every person who hears it kills themselves, I don't think. If it were, there'd be more than a few hundred deaths. But there really are countries where this song is banned from the airwaves."

"That sounds like something that has to do with mind control and hypnosis. I bet if you looked into it, you'd find some theories like that. I'll keep that in mind next time I need a story." It might be good to look it up when I had some free time.

"But it's really weird, isn't it, Gamotan?" Ryotasu must have been excited. Her cheeks were flushed

"Really? You can find urban legends about songs that make you kill yourself all over the world. It's not really that special."

"Not that! Why did your radio pick up that song?"

"Why? Oh, I see. I didn't really tune the dial anywhere, did I?" Normally you'd only hear white noise. She was probably asking why it just happened to pick up "Gloomy Sunday" now. Sure, that was a little odd, but...

"But I've seen stuff like this before. Sometimes you just happen to have the right shortwave frequency to pick up a broadcast from some country somewhere."

"That's not it!" Ryotasu was fidgeting in frustration. Her melons heaved in time with each fidget. "That's not it! Look, Gamotan. Your radio—" Ryotasu pointed to the power switch on the radio. "The power's off."

"Huh?" There was a switch that turned the power on and off. She was right. It was currently in the "off" position.

I didn't remember touching the switch since I'd opened the case, but I could still hear the song coming from the speakers anyway. Me, Myu-Pom, and Master Izumin all fell silent as we looked at it. The only sound in the quiet café was a woman's gloomy voice singing.

PARANORMAL SCIENCE NVL

Occultic;Nine

オカルティック・ナイン

THERE IS NO SUCH THING AS THE "OCCULT." IT CAN ALL BE DISPROVED BY SCIENCE.
ONLY THOSE WHO HAVE ACCEPTED EVERYTHING
HAVE THE RIGHT TO KNOW THE TRUTH.

"Our suspicions were correct, and some of the bug receptors are behaving unexpectedly."

"Unexpectedly?" Takasu put his teacup on the table, annoyed. "Even though it's been over a century since Tesla created this system?"

"Yes…"

Takasu moaned to himself and looked at the room's aquarium. It was lit up and filled with tropical fish, which were swimming peacefully, oblivious to Takasu's worries.

"We live in an era when most of theology can be explained with science. Why are we having so many problems with this?"

The fish, of course, did not answer.

THERE IS NO SUCH THING AS THE "OCCULT." IT CAN ALL BE DISPROVED BY SCIENCE.
ONLY THOSE WHO HAVE ACCEPTED EVERYTHING
HAVE THE RIGHT TO KNOW THE TRUTH.

▶ site 21: Toko Sumikaze ——— 2/22 (Monday)

I could hear birds chirping outside the window and squinted at the sunlight's glare as it came through the blinds. I tried my best to stifle a yawn.

"Hey, good morning." Takafuji, the editor-in-chief, came into the department office and began to greet everyone. I quickly jumped out of my chair.

"Sir, can you take a look at this?" I shoved the project plan that I'd spent the whole night working on in his face as he was still taking off his coat.

"Hey, Sumikaze. You been here all night? Can you start by getting me some coffee? I'm freezing." The editor-in-chief folded up his coat and tossed it on the desk, then motioned with his head toward the coffeepot in the corner.

"Sure. I can get you some coffee right away, but please read this."

"What is this?"

"It's the story you asked me to look into. It's a lot darker than I expected, so I wanted to spend some more pages on it."

He still looked skeptical, but I pushed the papers into his hands. Then, I hurried to the coffeepot. I poured the black liquid, brewing since yesterday, into a paper cup. Then I walked back to the editor-in-chief and put it in front of him as he read.

"This is the thing with the mummy and the girl, right? Weren't you whining about how you couldn't find anything occult about it?"

"I wasn't...whining." At least, I hadn't in front of him. I guess he'd heard me anyway.

"Hmm... Still, it's too late to give you more pages for this. We just decided at the last editors' meeting that our topic for next month's issue would be the flying humanoids of Mexico."

"Come on, don't be like that. Just give it a read, would you?"

"You want me to read all this? Just give me a summary."

"Oh, you'd prefer it that way?" That was just how I wanted it, too. Face-to-face, I could be *pretty* persuasive.

"Look at the second page." The image on the second page was a copy of an old newspaper article. It was from the society section, and it wasn't very big.

The headline read, "Live-Donor Kidney Transplant Fails in Tokyo, Donor Dies."

"This article is from three years ago. A kidney transplant was conducted at Tokyo Medical University in Hachioji, and due to malpractice, the donor died." The donor's name was Takaharu Minase, age 27.

"Malpractice? Did something like that happen?"

"It did. It never went to trial, but after the incident, *Yomikai Newspaper* did a big series of stories calling them out for medical malpractice. Remember?" Evidently, he didn't.

The kidney was to be transplanted from Takaharu Minase to his younger sister, Ria, who was just fourteen years old at the time.

"The transplant itself was a success. Her condition after the kidney transplant was just fine." The editor-in-chief silently motioned for me to continue.

This was where the true darkness behind the case began. "After the operation, Ria was unable to accept the death of her beloved brother. Several days later, Takaharu Minase's body disappeared from the hospital morgue. That day coincides with the day that Ria Minase left the hospital."

"Did she take the body with her?"

"Yes...at only fourteen years old, she snuck into a hospital morgue and stole her brother's body without anyone noticing. Or from her perspective, she took him home. She put him in a wheelchair and walked home."

"Hold on. Where was this hospital?"

"Hachioji."

The editor-in-chief fell silent at my answer. His eyes silently said, "Seriously?"

"She walked back to Kichijoji from Hachioji. That's 20 kilometers as the crow flies, and this girl was recovering from a kidney transplant and pushing her dead brother in a wheelchair."

" ... "

"And once she got back, she started to live with her brother's corpse. That's strange enough, but what's worse is that it took her relatives a full year to notice. Doesn't that just make you shiver?"

The dark side of the modern nuclear family, the collapse of Japan's village-oriented society... If you were to analyze this from a sociological perspective, you might use phrases like that.

But this family *certainly* wasn't normal. They were so obsessed with keeping up their noble outward appearance that they covered up the disappearance of the body. It vanished into the darkness without making the news or the police getting involved. They must've gone searching for it on their own, too.

That wasn't what interested me about this case, of course. "In the end, it was a year before her relatives found out about the body and took it away from her. Are you listening? 'Cause this is where it gets interesting."

I leaned forward. The editor-in-chief leaned away, obviously a little spooked. "Ria Minase still lives all alone in the same house. Now she's changed her name and runs something she calls a 'black magic agency.' The place is located in Harmonica Alley in Kichijoji. So, pop quiz. When you hear the words 'black magic' and 'mummy,' what's the first thing that comes to mind?"

He looked annoyed, and tossed the papers on the desk. "Listen to me, Sumikaze. What kind of magazine do you think *Mumuu* is?"

"Huh?"

"We're not a gossip rag." He sighed deeply and took a sip from his coffee, then winced. It must've been more bitter than he was expecting.

"For one thing, where's the occult in that story you just told me? It just sounds like a crazy girl acting crazy."

"Well, the plan is to talk about Aria Kurenaino—that's what Ria Minase calls herself now. I know she's trying to use her black magic to do something."

"Sumikaze." He glared at me. There was a piercing light in his eyes. "I told you to look into this case, but only insofar as we could find something to use for a *Mumuu* article. If you really want to do this, go find proof that this Aria girl can 'cause supernatural events to happen with her magic,' and bring that to me. That's all."

"What? Ascension, sir! That's too harsh!"

"Come on, I'm being nice. Sheesh... This is the problem with kids these days."

"When you call someone a kid, it's because you're actually a kid yourself." *Well, maybe I should be glad he didn't tell me to kill the whole story.* "All right. I'll go over this all again."

I took back the papers and reluctantly headed back to my seat. There was some truth to what he said. Instead of staying cooped up in the office and thinking, it felt like I needed to get out there and dig deeper. Otherwise, I wasn't a journalist. I was just an amateur.

"So what should I do now?" With my tension gone, I was starting to feel really sleepy.

I bit back another yawn and wiped away the tears that were forming in my eyes, then looked out at the blue winter sky that peeked through the gaps in the blinds.

I wondered to myself...

What did the world look like to Aria Kurenaino? She was insane. I knew it. So what did she see? And—

What did she *hear?*

PARANORMAL SCIENCE NVL

Occultic;Nine
オカルティック・ナイン

THERE IS NO SUCH THING AS THE "OCCULT." IT CAN ALL BE DISPROVED BY SCIENCE.
ONLY THOSE WHO HAVE ACCEPTED EVERYTHING
HAVE THE RIGHT TO KNOW THE TRUTH.

Yuta Gamon, or Gamo, was a type of person I'd never encountered before.

Calling him an otaku wouldn't be quite right. I had some otaku in my class, but he was more—to put it quite bluntly—obnoxious.

Right now, he was muttering to himself as he fiddled with the switches on that radio he always carried around. It kind of looked like he was talking to it.

"What I'm saying here is that we need something with more impact than just an ordinary interview. Maybe we should just have Kirikiri Basara take over 'Myu's Niconico Live Fortune-Telling.' The best option would be to have her do a photo shoot in a bikini, but that's no different than your average idol, and it's not fair to ask an amateur to go that far. Hint, hint."

"You don't have to hint. It's not happening." I ignored him and took a sip of the "Prototype Ultra-Lucky Mango Lassi" that Master Izumi had just brought me. A sweet and sour taste filled my mouth. *Oh, wow! This is really good. I don't know what's lucky about it, though.*

Gamo must have been shocked by my cold refusal, because he sank into the sofa and sulked.

Whenever he asked for something, it was always crazy, but when I told him no, he always quickly dropped it. He was a little wimpier than I thought he would be. Maybe he was afraid of someone not liking him.

In other words...he was only tough on the internet? "I know, I know. This is just my personal wish, or maybe what I'm imagining. I mean, of course, I've imagined you wearing a swimsuit, but that doesn't mean I'd actually want you to do it. I'm not an idol producer or anything. But I know there's demand for photos of you in a bikini. You know it, baby."

"Don't call me 'baby.'" And anyway, it was winter. You'd have to be an idiot to wear a swimsuit when it was this cold out.

I felt cold pretty easily, so to me, that'd be suicide. My body temperature dropped just thinking about it. It felt like I was going to start to shiver, so I pulled my hoodie over my head. I didn't like the cold.

"Man, what's the best way to do this? The nuance is really important here. Depending on the way we tell everybody that you're working for us now, we could get loads of praise or start a huge flame war. If we make it look like me and Myu-Pom are too close, the fans will get jealous, and the eggs on Twitter will start coming after me. Just me, you see. I want to avoid that."

"I don't think I've got that many passionate fans. I'm not really an idol or anything."

"You don't get it! You don't understand your own popularity at all." Gamo pointed his index finger right at my face in frustration.

I wish he wouldn't point at people like that.

"Dancers and singers on Nico get a ton of attention! There's even scandals involving them. You've got a ton of views on your account, and you've been on TV, too. You've got dozens of times more fans than your average idol. I know it!"

"Huh..." *He probably doesn't have to worry about any of that,* I thought.

Still, he sure liked to talk...

When I first met him at school, he was much more awkward. Like, I'd never seen a boy so shy.

When he talked, he always sounded so wimpy, too.

It was pretty tiring to listen to him, maybe.

Would being with him really open up the future? It's not like I doubted my own power, but he didn't look like the kind of person who would open up the future for me. I was feeling super-nervous.

"Gamotan, you're worrying too much!" Narusawa, who had been dancing around the room and singing, said to him. Her huge breasts wobbled as she spoke. Those things were so big that, even as a girl, I couldn't help but stare.

"You used to update Kirikiri Basara every day, but you haven't for days! Everybody's waiting for your update! They're waiting! Ting! Ting!"

"She's right. I've seen comments from people worried about you." Gamo's eyes went wide.

"Huh? The Basariters are worried about me? Seriously? I thought they hated me, but they don't! Man, I feel like I'm going to cry!" "Basariters" was his nickname for people who commented on Kirikiri Basara. They wrote negative comments about the occult beneath his articles. Their specialized knowledge was what made Kirikiri Basara such a unique site! ...At least, that's what Gamo had told me.

"So what are the comments like, Myu-Pom?" It was hard to answer when he was staring at me with those shining, puppy-dog eyes, but...

Was it okay to tell him?

"Most of them said things like, 'The admin's out of stuff to talk about? Buh-bye.'"

Gamo said, "They're not worried at all," and slumped onto the table.

"Screw 'em. Screw the Basariters. I've got stuff to talk about. And you Basariters have been a bunch of wimps lately. The number of comments hasn't gone up at all! And I haven't seen Sarai show up once since Myu-Pom wrecked him."

That's because none of your articles are any good... is what I almost said, but I stopped myself at the last second.

"Oh, you just thought that my articles were boring, didn't you?"

"Me? That's not...*ah ah aha*..." I tried to laugh it off, but...I don't think I did a very good job.

"The reason we're not getting many comments is that all the articles on you are breaking news." There were three articles on me up on the site right now.

"The Whole Internet's Talking About Teenage Fortune-Teller Myu Aikawa." That was an aggregator article about me. And then there was last week's advertisement post that was uploaded just before my livestream.

After that, there was another ad for me, about the TV program I was on.

"True, but except for the first one, they're breaking news articles.

They're interesting when they happen, but maybe not interesting later."

"That's why the hit counter went crazy after they were uploaded, but it didn't last. We need something more like a 'Myu Aikawa Special' that's still worth going back to later. Which is why that swimsuit photo shoot—"

"It's *not* happening." Who knew if anybody would want to read an article about me, anyway?

Gamo thought I was a lot more special than I really was.

"At this rate, Kirikiri Basara is doomed! ☆ Saraba Basara! ♪ Saraba Basara! ♪ " Narusawa was singing and dancing.

Did she get that from when I'd messed the name up? "All right, Ryotasu, go interview Professor Hashigami for us then. Remember how I just made you Special Correspondent?"

"Pohyahyah?"

"The new school year starts in April, so he's gonna be busy, right? This is our chance."

"Correspondent! ☆ Correspondent! ☆ Correspondents get the best deals! Yesterday they gave me half-off oranges at the fruit stand in Harmonica Alley! It was such a good deal that I bought a whole box! ☆ So now my fingers have been orange all day! ☆ "

"No, um... Ryotasu? I'm not talking about oranges." Gamo was seriously weird, but Narusawa was even weirder.

She would start singing or dancing, or saying weird things out of nowhere, but at times, she could be astonishingly perceptive. But it also felt like she basically never listened to what anyone else had to say.

An...unusual girl like her would be sure to make waves at school. But I'd never heard anybody talk about her in the year or so since I'd started going to that school. I couldn't remember passing by her in

253

the hallway, either.

Maybe she was pretending to be a different kind of person at school? If she was, maybe she was like me. Like how I was both Miyuu and Myu.

"Come on, Gamotan, sniff my fingers. You'll go 'Waaah!'"

"Hey, stop it!"

Man, those two are really close. They started messing around the minute you let your guard down. Maybe it was more accurate to say that Narusawa was messing with Gamo.

It was hard for a newcomer like me to interrupt them. And actually, it was really hard to say anything when they were flirting with each other like that.

Was I overthinking things? I didn't want to spend the whole day just sitting here talking about nothing. We were supposed to be here to figure out Kirikiri Basara's future plans. But Gamo kept worrying about the same thing over and over. And Narusawa was just playing around, and not really participating in the conversation.

We weren't going to get anywhere like this.

"Um..."

"Mmm?"

So, I decided to interrupt them and ask a "new girl" question. "Is there some kind of rule that Kirikiri Basara uses to pick the articles it writes? You don't talk about things that are old, or that happen outside Japan, right?"

"That's right. If we wrote about old stuff, we'd just be another page about urban legends. There's a ton of those already."

"So that means it's fine as long as it's new?"

"It can't just be new, though. First, it has to happen in Japan.

Especially somewhere near the Chuo rail line in Tokyo. Ideally, it's something that happens in Kichijoji." That was a pretty narrow range, then.

"Why?"

"It makes it easier to go investigate it. Make sense?"

"Myu..." I immediately regretted asking a serious question.

"But Gamotan, Gamotan, you've never actually gone anywhere to investigate an article for Kirikiri Basara."

"Umm... That's because we've never really had to." In other words, he was just lazy. He might not have been taking this web site as seriously as I thought.

I gave him a look that said "Work harder," but he refused to look at me. *Grr... Do your job!*

"Um, also, we avoid things that are too complicated and hard to follow. I mean, if you write something complicated, only smart people can read it, right? That's a terrible way to get hits. I want something that idiots can read." The real reason was probably that he was too lazy to look stuff up. No, not probably. Definitely. I was starting to get a feel for who Gamo really was.

But at the same time, he was probably right. I'd read most of the articles on Kirikiri Basara over the past few days, and they were all quick reads that were easy to understand. That was probably really important.

"Also, there's one thing that's more important than anything else when I'm deciding what to write about on Kirikiri Basara." *One thing?* Gamo paused dramatically, then looked at me, and then Ryotasu, and finally, toward Master Izumin behind the counter.

"Hey, Gamota. Why are you staring at me? Did you fall in love?

Sorry. I'm not into guys, heheh."

You're lying, I thought to myself. But I didn't say it.

Gamo said, "You're lying," in a voice so small I could barely hear it, and then made a "bleh" sound.

"You're lying! ☆" Narusawa said, and then she started to dance.

Nobody really wanted to find out if he was lying or not, though, so we didn't say anything more. As for Narusawa's dance show...I decided to ignore that.

"What's the most important thing?"

"How easy is it for the Basariters to rip things apart?" "Rip it apart" was a phrase that I saw used all the time on Kirikiri Basara. It meant to scientifically and logically disprove something...supposedly.

"So it's best if it just seems a little shady. If it's too serious, or too obviously a fake, it doesn't do as well."

"I see... I wouldn't have thought of that."

"Gamotan's amazing, huh? He's really thought about this."

"I may not look it, but I'm a very popular blogger. Or at least, trying to be one." Gamo stuck out his chest.

But—

"Does that mean that you think I'm a little shady too?"

"Oh, uh..." Gamo started to fidget and glance around the room.

"You're trying to have the Basariters cut me up, aren't you? That's really mean!"

"No, no, wait. Your articles are different..."

I chuckled. "I was just kidding," I said.

And it didn't really matter to me what the Basariters thought. It would be kind of a shock if they were mean to me, and I might cry again, but I believed in my power. My goal wasn't to be a famous fortune-teller.

"Hey, hey, Gamotan. How long is Kirikiri Basara going to stay shut down?"

"Ryotasu, I can't remember you ever looking forward to Kirikiri Basara's updates that much."

"Sometimes there's something that's always there, and then it goes away, right? That's when you realize how important it was to you. ☆" Even listening to her say that made me blush, and she said it with a big smile on her face. Narusawa was cute, but there was something else about her, too.

Gamo must've felt embarrassed too, because he was blushing bright red.

"I've got a stock of things to write about piled up. I've been so busy thinking about Myu-Pom that I haven't updated the site, that's all." That's what he said, but it sounded like an excuse.

"What do you have, for example?"

"I'm warming up an article on that 'Gloomy Sunday' song I heard from my radio."

"Ding! ☆ It's all warmed up! ☆"

Come to think of it, he'd said he still didn't know what had caused that.

That was crazy, wasn't it? A song, playing from a radio when the power was off. Me, Gamo, Narusawa, and Master Izumin had all heard it, and none of us knew what the cause was.

In the end, we'd just settled on Gamo's radio being broken that day. No one had ever come up with a better explanation.

I suddenly remembered the song's melody, and shivered. Maybe it was better not to think about it too much.

"Samurai Gamonosuke? Is there anything else you're warming up?" Gamo grinned in answer to her question.

He moved the radio to the side of the table and got out his laptop.

"Well for example, they say that God appears at Inokashira Park. Mostly on weekday afternoons." He was saying something really weird.

"Ahaha, God appears at the park? And only on weekday afternoons? Man, that's hilarious."

"It's not a joke. God doesn't show up often, but it does happen."

"Wow! I want to meet God!"

"Does it have something to do with that torii arch or something?" There was a shrine to the god Benzaiten next to the lake in Inokashira Park. I think I remembered going there with Dad when I was little.

But Gamo shook his head. "Oh, it's not a serious god like that."

I didn't know that there was such a thing as a non-serious god.

"It's a self-proclaimed god."

"Huh? What do you mean?"

"Okay, got it. I'll put this as plainly as I can. The best way to describe him is... He's a homeless guy, probably."

Wait. Seriously? That was lame.

According to Gamo, this self-proclaimed god would appear at the park sometimes on weekday afternoons, and give crazy speeches in a loud voice.

"There's threads on 2ch that follow him. He says stuff about the world's destruction starting in Musashino or something. He's one of those 'I have to save the world from a conspiracy theory' types of nuts."

"Can I see him, too?"

"It'd be hard for a student to go on a weekday afternoon. There's no real schedule for when he appears, too. The day of the week and time are mostly random. Some days, he doesn't show up at all."

So, we'd just have to hope we ran into him by chance, huh?

"So once spring break came around, I was going to go looking for God. You know, if we had an article titled 'Interview with God!' it would get a ton of hits."

"Wouldn't the Basariters get mad at you? You'd be tricking them."

"Haha, you don't get it! You don't get it at all, Myu-Pom." He sighed at me in irritation. It was kind of aggravating to have someone mock me so openly.

"You never heard of the Bourbon House threads on 2ch? It's the same thing as that. There's kind of an unspoken harmony between the people who trick someone with a thread title and the people who enjoy being tricked. Knowing the Basariters, they'd love it."

Is that how it works?

"Hey, instead of covering that weird god, let me give you a special local story." Master Izumin had finished wiping his glasses. He came out from behind the bar and grinned.

"A friend told me about this weird shop they found in Harmonica Alley."

Harmonica Alley was a tiny little shopping street near Kichijoji Station. Most of the place was bars, so it was busy morning and night.

"Harmonica Alley, huh?" Gamo reacted immediately.

"Is that the House of Crimson?"

"Oh, yeah! That's the name of it! Gamota, did you know about it?"

"Who do you think I am? I'm the admin of Kirikiri Basara, the NEET God himself. That's one of the other stories I've got warming up on the pile. Let me see here—" Gamo started to fiddle with the touch pad on his PC.

"Here it is. This place, right?" He turned the LCD screen of the laptop toward Master Izumin, with another big grin on his face.

I saw a black background, with "The House of Crimson" written in bright red letters.

It looked like he was displaying the store's homepage on an internet browser.

"Yes, that's it!"

"What kind of place is it?" Gamo tilted his head a little in confusion.

"A black magic agency... or something." He didn't sound very confident.

"An agency?"

"I don't really know. Master Izumin, do you know anything?"

"They place curses on people with black magic, supposedly. I heard that unless you bring them a lock of hair from whoever you want cursed, they won't accept the job."

"Huh... I'll write that down." Gamo started to tap at the keyboard excitedly.

Hmm... Cursing people, huh? Could you really make a living doing that? Were there a lot of people in the world who wanted to curse someone?

That was really bad, right? Just imagining it made me want to shiver. If someone put a curse on you like that without you knowing, how could you protect yourself? Since I had my power to see "visions," it was kind of hard for me to laugh the idea off.

"Anyway, if they need hair, shouldn't they be putting that on the homepage? Are they serious about this? Do they think anybody's going to come to their store these days without even the tiniest bit of explanation? And what do they need hair for, anyway? Don't tell me the devil's going to run a DNA test." As he typed the information into his PC's notepad program, he seemed to be mad about something I didn't really understand.

"But you know, Gamota, wouldn't that keep out people who weren't serious? Only people who really want to curse someone would come to the store, right? It's pretty hard to get somebody else's hair, you know."

"What kind of reputation does the House of Crimson have?"

"Oh, yeah! Get this!" Master Izumin sat down in a chair. He seemed intent on joining in the conversation. He looked like a musclebound man, but he was acting like a gossipy old lady. "A friend of a friend said that somebody got hit by a car because of one of their curses!"

"Wow, you're kidding me. The minute you said the words 'friend of a friend,' my trust in your story plummeted to zero."

"What do you mean, zero?! Are you saying I don't have any friends?"

"You said 'a friend of a friend,' but the question is how many friends you're skipping in between." Gamo was shaking his head, as if he couldn't believe Master Izumin didn't understand something so simple. Sometimes he could be really self-confident and kind of a jerk.

"'A friend of a friend' makes it sound like somebody close to you, but it might be a friend of a friend of a friend of a friend of a friend of a friend of a friend of a friend of a friend, right?" he continued. "Everyone knows not to trust 'friend of a friend' stories. That's an old rule." It felt like I was hearing an incantation from another world. I wished he wouldn't repeat the word "friend" so much.

"Oh, I see." Master Izumin looked super-ticked. But he quickly smiled mischievously.

"By the way, this is something else a friend of a friend told me, but the owner of this black magic agency is supposed to be a pretty, young girl."

"What...did you say?" I thought I saw a different glint in Gamo's eyes.

Didn't he just say he didn't believe friends of friends?

"So that's got you interested, huh? You're shy, Gamo, but you love girls, don't you?"

"O-of course I like them. But don't get the wrong idea! I'm not some man-slut pickup artist. I don't really want to date a real girl or anything. Definitely don't get the wrong idea."

"Really?"

"That's right. I'm a NEET God, for one thing. But if the black magic agent who's cursing people turned out to be a pretty, young girl, wouldn't that be cool? It's not every day you run into a girl who ticks that many boxes. If I write about her on Kirikiri Basara, it'll mean a ton of new hits. And all that affiliate money, too!"

"Hmph... Gamo, you're even worse than I thought—" I huffed.

"Hmm? Worse than you thought how?"

"No, I won't say it," I chuckled.

He was even more easy to please than I thought he was. But that didn't mean he was an idiot. He'd said something similar when I'd joined Kirikiri Basara's staff. In a way, he was consistent. I couldn't respect him, but I could feel that he was acting in accordance with his beliefs.

"Still, you know... Black magic? Devils? If there really were something like that, I'd want to be friends with it." Gamo continued.

"That would be kind of cool. It would make me more popular as a blogger, right? Man, I want to see a devil. I really want to see a devil."

I could see Narusawa slowly creeping up behind him. Our eyes met, and she put her finger to her lips as if to say "Shhhh!" Gamo hadn't noticed her.

What was she doing? I watched, excitedly.

Narusawa pinched a few strands of his hair with her pretty fingers.

"Huh?"

"Pluck? Pluck! ☆" And then she yanked them out, hard.

"Ow!" As Gamo writhed in pain, I could see ten or so strands of hair in Narusawa's hands.

"Hey, what are you doing, Ryotasu?"

"I'm your correspondent, right?"

"Huh?"

"Pan-paka-pan! Correspondent Ryotasu is off to do her duty!" Narusawa raised Gamo's hair high above her head.

"Um, where are you going?"

"You know where I'm going, silly! Somewhere I can use this hair! ☆"

"You don't mean..." Narusawa pointed her finger toward Gamo's laptop.

"Black Magic Papacy! Bam! Ba-bam!"

Agency, you mean...

"Wait, why is today the only day you actually want to work? Is it the Myu-Pom Effect?" Gamo looked confused.

"Why me?"

"I mean, you know how in anime and manga, there's always rivals. You two could be trying to show off to me, to show which of you is really the true Basara Girl."

I understood that a Basara Girl was like a Bond Girl, but I wasn't interested in being one at all.

"Anyway, Ryotasu, can you give me back my hair?"

"But isn't this your big chance, Gamo?" I suggested.

"Huh? How so?"

"If your hair gets you cursed by a devil, you'll get your chance to become friends with one, right?"

"Oh, um... Y-yeah. I am the NEET God, after all. *Ah ha ha*... By the way, Ryotasu, are you really not going to give me back my hair? Why don't we go to Woodberrys right now? My treat?" Gamo's face was twitching.

Aha ha!

Narusawa refused, saying only, "I'm a correspondent!" After that, she moved super-fast.

Maybe she's this fast because she's used to ignoring what everyone else wants, I thought to myself as I stared up at the sign for Harmonica Alley.

"We're here! ☆" I still couldn't believe we'd visited the shop that very day. Talk about super-bold.

"Maybe I'll go home... I'm so nervous, my stomach is hurting." It wasn't that bad during the livestreams, but now my heart was pounding in a really weird way.

"Nope! ☆ Myu, you're part of Kirikiri Basara, too! ☆ Kirikiri! Come on, Kirikiri! ☆" Narusawa made a cute pose at me in front of the crowded entrance to Harmonica Alley.

The people's stares as they passed by were physically painful. If anything felt like it was getting ripped apart, it was my stomach.

The sun had already set. Harmonica Alley's cramped street was filled with salarymen on their way home from work.

I always passed by this place on my way home from school, but I'd never actually gone inside.

I was a minor, so there was no reason for me to go there. And I had this weird idea that if I did, I might get creeped on by middle-aged drunk guys.

Narusawa had been in such a hurry that I hadn't even had time to change out of my school uniform. That worried me, too. I felt totally out of place. If any of the teachers saw me here, they were sure to get mad at me. And if the police saw me and took me in, that would be even worse. Narusawa wasn't wearing her uniform, and if you didn't look too closely—or closely at all, really—she could kind of pass for an adult.

"Alright! Time for me to become a drunk! ☆ Mumuu!" Narusawa started to pretend to stagger around like a drunk.

Was this really okay? The only reason I'd come was because I was worried about her being here alone. I'd told Gamo he should come too, but...

"I'm the one who's going to be cursed. If I come too, there's no point." He'd given that excuse and refused to come. It was plainly obvious that he was scared.

I'd come along since I didn't have a choice, but...Umyu! I couldn't stay standing here forever! It was do or die time, maybe!

"Okay, let's go!" I motioned for Narusawa to follow me and stepped into Harmonica Alley.

I'd memorized the map of the alley after looking it up online. We took the shortest route to our destination, the House of Crimson.

When we arrived, all we found was a tiny sign and a plain-looking entrance. The sign only read, "Black Magic Agency—The House of Crimson." If someone came here without knowing anything about it, they'd be too scared to get close. Especially since going inside meant walking up a gloomy, dimly lit staircase.

I looked up the stairs. There was a door at the top. I could see the dim light of the shop from the small window.

"Okay, Narusawa. All ready? Okay? Just follow the plan."

"Yup. ☆" Narusawa grinned and gave a little cheer.

This was the plan: Narusawa and I were supposedly both in a relationship with Gamo, who was cheating on us both. But when we'd talked about it with each other, we'd decided that we'd put a curse on him to make him pay for what he'd done. Gamo had come up with this plan.

I'd said that I personally didn't like it, because it made Gamo out to be much more popular with girls than he really was. He'd gotten mad and told me to come up with my own plan, then.

"Knock, knock, knock! ☆" Narusawa went up the stairs first. They were so steep that I could see up her skirt from where I was standing.

I looked around to make sure there were no men nearby, and then sighed. Narusawa needed to be way more careful. *Could you believe it? Normally, you'd at least try to hide that.*

"Hello! ☆" Narusawa opened the door with a laid-back greeting.

I followed right after her. "Come on, don't greet her like that..." There was no way the owner would believe that we were poor girls who'd been cheated on now.

I felt like the plan was already blown, but I followed her up the stairs anyway. Of course, I kept a close eye on the hem of my skirt.

The inside of the shop had a ceiling that was a little low, but it wasn't as cramped as the staircase. Since it was a black magic shop, there wasn't much light, and there were all kinds of creepy merchandise everywhere.

Wow...this place really *felt* evil.

Black magic and fortune-telling might seem similar, but they were totally different. All these different tools were meaningless to me, and I didn't really like places like this that were supposed to feel mystic and foreboding. I always wanted my fortune-telling to be cheerful and fun.

It felt kind of hard to breathe, maybe. It felt like being underwater.

"Welcome to the House of Crimson." I suddenly gasped as I heard a voice speak to me.

She sat silently in the back of the store.

She was very pretty. That's how it felt to me, from the bottom of my heart. She was really pretty. She had long black hair, elegant features, and a sad expression. It was like looking at a doll, somehow.

Was she the store owner that people were talking about? Oh, wow, she was a lot younger than I thought. Was she maybe not that much older than me?

The owner of the store stood up and brought us chairs from the corner of the shop. "Please, sit down."

Narusawa and I sat down across from her. I didn't want to stare, but she was just so pretty that I couldn't help myself. Narusawa sat next to me, her eyes shining as she looked at the five stuffed animals on the shelves behind the girl.

"They're so cute! ☆" She hadn't forgotten the plan, had she?

The girl poured us herbal tea. I thanked her and took a sip, and sighed as it warmed my body.

The owner of the store said her name was Aria Kurenaino.

"This is your first visit, isn't it?" She began to explain her system as a black magic agent.

She told us that her "dolls," the super-cute stuffed animals on her shelf, would do the actual work of cursing someone for us. She told us that there were three packages, depending on the price we wanted to pay. And that the more expensive the package, the more effective the curse.

There was no way for me to know how much of what she was saying was real and how much was fake, but the idea of stuffed animals carrying out the curse made things seem a little less brutal for the client, and maybe a little easier.

"Which package will you choose?" All three packages were expensive. For a student like me, even the cheapest package was expensive.

Narusawa didn't seem like she'd listened to the explanation. She just stared at the dolls, and answered without a hint of hesitation.

"I'll take the Devil's Ritual! ☆"

"What?" She picked that not because of the price, but the number of dolls! The Devil's Ritual used all five dolls, but it was the most expensive, at 66,600 yen.

With Aria sitting right there, I couldn't say anything about it, so I just sat there in shock.

And I couldn't believe my eyes when I saw Narusawa take almost 70,000 yen out of her wallet. Was she really going to pay 66,600 yen?

Was Narusawa from a really rich family or something, maybe? Why would a girl like that be hanging out with Gamo?

"Understood." Aria took the money and slowly nodded.

She spread out a sheet with a magic symbol drawn on it on the table. And then she put the five dolls on top of the symbol.

Narusawa poked the green-striped doll in front of her on the head with her finger. I was terrified that Aria might get mad at her.

"So what's your request?" Aria didn't smile, but that only made her seem more alluring and beautiful.

It felt like she really could use black magic.

"Samurai Gamonosuke cheated on me! ☆ Please curse him for me! Thanks! ☆"

"*Aha ha...* um... Narusawa? I don't know if she'll be able to understand that."

"Poyah?"

Don't say "Poyah."

I figured that even Aria must have been confused by that, but when I looked, her expression hadn't changed.

But even if her expression hadn't changed, her tiny white hands grabbed one of the dolls—a weird-looking one with a white bag on its head that she called Lilith XII—and began to fiddle with it. That was her only reaction.

Was she trying not to laugh or get mad?

"Um... I think we should explain it better... We were, ummm..." I tried to think of a nicer way to put it, but I gave up.

"Let's try to explain more about the man who cheated on us, okay?" I whispered in her ear, and Narusawa put her finger to her cheek and began to stare at the ceiling. But she only made that thinking pose for a second.

"Gamotan is a year older than me. He's also a year older than Myu.

We became friends two days ago! ☆" Aria's hands began to move faster as she played with Lilith XII. If it could speak, it might have been screaming in pain.

"Um, so you see..." I interrupted. "There's a man named Yuta Gamon, and he was cheating on me and Narusawa here. And he calls me Myu-Pom, too. And so we talked about it, and we decided that we were going to make him pay."

"..."

The only sound in the room was my voice echoing off the thin walls. Why did I feel so tense?

Aria wasn't looking at us. She was looking down at the boy- (or maybe girl-) doll in her hands. She still had no expression on her face. I couldn't tell what she was thinking.

I couldn't tell.

Was it a good idea to explain things like I just did, anyway?

I gave her Gamo's name. What if she really cursed him? I couldn't tell.

I was really worried. What was I doing here? Was it a good idea to test her like this? I didn't know.

I didn't know, so I couldn't help but look...at a vision of Aria.

Open, Yesod.

I didn't actually have the cards in front of me, and without them, the visions were less clear, but...

I imagined them in my mind.

I imagined myself flipping over the 9th card. That was all I had to do.

That was all it took for the vision to appear.

I saw a dimly lit place that looked like it was filled with fog. There were countless silhouettes of people floating around me.

I was beneath dirty water. The filthy mud floating up from the bottom cut off the moonlight on the surface.

No way... This was...

"Myu?"

"Myu?!" I came back to my senses.

Narusawa had her hand on my shoulder and was looking at me, worried.

"I-I'm sorry...I'm fine." I shook my head and tried to forget about the vision I'd just seen. I felt someone looking at me.

Aria had raised her head and was staring at me. I had to say something.

"I-I was so shocked... It was such a shock that he was cheating on me..." My voice was shaking, but I think that helped me fool her, maybe.

"I understand. Then I will now perform the ceremony." Aria's voice was firm.

Evidently, she'd believed us. Afterward, I watched in silence as Aria performed some kind of black magic ritual.

But later, I couldn't remember what she did at all. I was thinking of something else the whole time.

My vision of Aria... the way she was down at the bottom of the water.

I'd seen the same vision before. It was when I'd tried to find the livestreamer who'd done One-Man Hide and Seek.

Why? Did she have something to do with the man who'd gone missing? Or was he killed by her curse? I was terrified, and my whole body was freezing. I clutched my arms tightly around myself until the ritual was over. I wanted to get out of this shop as soon as possible.

I didn't have the courage to speak or to stop the ceremony, so the contract to curse Gamo was made.

PARANORMAL SCIENCE NVL

Occultic;Nine

THERE IS NO SUCH THING AS THE "OCCULT." IT CAN ALL BE DISPROVED BY SCIENCE.
ONLY THOSE WHO HAVE ACCEPTED EVERYTHING
HAVE THE RIGHT TO KNOW THE TRUTH.

▶ site 23: MMG

"Things have been awfully noisy lately." The voice came from the back of the room, in an area blocked off by curtains. The voice was calm and emotionless, but Takasu could feel a tension running through his mind and body as it spoke.

"Yes...there were more problems with the first generation." He just barely managed to get the words out.

The back of the room was dimly lit, and from where he was standing, he couldn't see the speaker. The speaker kept talking, unconcerned with Takasu's fears. "Its specifications are so powerful, and yet you still can't fully master them? As you're aware, the first generation was still in the beta test stage. There's a variation in the overall scandium distribution. We're also seeing patterns where the receptors are causing extreme variation in brain activity. It's probably due to a mismatch with the receptor proteins, we believe."

"Orphan receptors, huh?" Takasu sighed, being careful not to let it be heard. There was no one besides this man who could scare him like this.

"We're still analyzing it, but despite the extreme similarity in amino acid arrangement, we're seeing what are clearly different results than the known protein receptors. It's a near certainty."

"And that's the cause of the bug receptors?"

"Yes. Most likely."

It felt like talking to the darkness, Takasu thought. A bottomless darkness. He wanted to get as close as possible to its depths. He wanted to live up to the expectations of the great person within it.

He was nervous, but talking to the voice was also Takasu's greatest joy. "The system protocol control continues to be unstable. If you wish to speak strictly in terms of 'specs,' they aren't too low..." Takasu paused to gulp down his saliva.

"They're too high."

I checked the time on my phone, and it was 5:12 PM. I looked up. The hallway was long and straight. I looked down toward the end.

There wasn't much light, both because the sun was about to set and because several lights had been turned off to save electricity. It felt a little like something out of a horror movie.

"The professor's not here after all..." I'd only wanted to whisper to myself, but my voice echoed more than I thought it would. I quickly looked around.

Building #10 was where the professors had their personal offices. It was the tallest building at Seimei University, I thought.

I was in a hallway on the sixth floor. There was no one here but me. Finals had just ended, it seemed, and so most of the students had probably gone home. But even accounting for that, the place shouldn't have been this empty.

I hadn't seen a single person since I'd come into the building.

Man, I want to go home. I really should go home.

I was wearing my high school uniform, so I felt really awkward.

This school was for scientists. If someone saw me wandering around, they'd be sure to ask me what I was doing.

"How did this happen?" It was all thanks to Ryotasu that I ended up here.

Two days ago, Ryotasu had suddenly shown a willingness to actually do work for once. She'd run off to do research on the black magic agency. My plan had been to take this newly awakened Ryotasu and have her go interview Dr. Hashigami for me.

When I went to go home from school today, Ryotasu, who I almost never saw at school, ambushed me at the entrance.

"Samurai Gamonosuke ☆, don't you think it's time you visited the professor? Like, right now?"

For my part, I thought visiting the professor without an appointment might be considered rude, so I tried to get out of it. But "Awakened Ryotasu" was a lot more pushy than usual.

"You should go! ☆ If you don't, you won't be able to see him! ☆ Now's your chance to stop being such a wimp-o-nosuke! ☆"

And so, well, I ended up reluctantly coming all the way to school.

The problem was, I was sure that Ryotasu would follow me, and she didn't. When we got to the entrance of the university, my self-proclaimed servant familiar said, "'Kay, good luck!" and headed straight home.

How could she make me do this by myself? Sure, I agree that it wasn't right for me to sit on my butt when my self-proclaimed servant familiar was working really hard. It would be a bad example not just for her, but for our newest member, Myu-Pom.

"But still, you know...I can't just show up for an interview without an appointment, right?" I muttered. If an average, boring high school student like me just showed up and asked for an interview, a professor who was famous enough to be on TV would never accept it.

In fact, he might say, "Get lost, trash."

My people skills weren't very good to begin with. A sudden interview was out of the question.

And I'd looked at the bulletin board on my way here, and Dr. Hashigami's seminar was closed for two weeks. That's why he wasn't here today. That bulletin board was what had told me how to find his lab, though.

"The professor's not here. I'll just take one quick look inside to make sure, and go home," I said. I could tell Ryotasu that I couldn't find him. It wouldn't be an excuse. It would be true, and it wouldn't be my fault. It wouldn't be my fault at all.

And so, I decided to stop hesitating and take a step toward the lab.

I was interested in what the professor had to say.

Mostly for my own personal reasons, though.

First, there was my fortune-telling princess, Myu-Pom, and then now Dr. Hashigami, who'd switched from denying the occult to believing in it.

With these two on my side, Kirikiri Basara would be the king of occult affiliate blogs. It was only a matter of time before I became as popular as *Mumuu Magazine* or *Tokyo Sports Newspaper*.

In other words, I would win! Forever! I'd have all the affiliate money I could ever spend! I could make enough money to live the NEET lifestyle, and do nothing but sleep all day! Work was for losers!

And my future was looking bright. Maybe I could make things a little easier for Mom, too.

But if I wanted to do this, I needed to make an appointment in advance and decide on my questions first. Then I'd have to come up with an article outline, and also decide whether to pay him for his time, or tell him that we couldn't pay him, and ask if that was okay. And I'd need to bring everybody, not just me.

That's how big this guy was. Ryotasu didn't understand that. *Yeah.* When it came right down to it, I was spooked.

"Wait, even if the professor's not here, someone from his seminar might be..." Not that I was 100% sure what a seminar was, though.

I had the image in my mind that even if the professor wasn't here, in a lab like this, one of his students might be up here working all night. If there were people here, what should I say?

And finally I made it to the door of Dr. Hashigami's lab. It was open a little, and I could see light coming from inside.

The hallway was cold. Didn't the draft coming into the room bother them? Or maybe it was warm enough inside that they just didn't care.

Man, this sucks. But I had to go in anyway, and so I knocked, softly. No answer.

Next, I knocked a little louder, but there was still no answer.

I took a look inside the room from the gap in the door. There was no noise. No sign of someone moving around. It was so quiet I thought my ears would hurt.

Was there nobody here, even though the lights were on? I opened the door and took a look inside the room.

"Excuse me..." I said.

Oddly enough, there was no one inside the room. Had they left the door half-open, and the lights on, while they went to the bathroom? "They should be more careful." Was this normal at a university? Either way, it felt stupid to be so nervous.

Anyway, I was a bit surprised at what I saw in the seminar room.

Compared to the image of Dr. Hashigami I saw on TV, it was plain and undecorated. It felt like a place that was being used for research. I'd expected him to like things a lot flashier.

It wasn't that big, either. It was honestly a little small, when you considered that his students would have to work here too.

In the center of the room were four desks. I wasn't sure if they were for his assistants, or his students.

The desks were cluttered with papers and other things. They really needed to clean this place up.

The walls were lined with shelves that reached all the way to the ceiling. The shelves were stacked with files and books. I could see issues of *Mumuu*, the magazine where the professor's column ran. There were also rows of books about Cthulhu, ghosts, aliens, and other occult topics. For a moment, I wasn't sure if this was really a university professor's office. A lot of this stuff was even worse than what you'd find on my bookshelves.

There was another door in the back that led to another room. This one was shut tight.

"Oh..." Maybe they were in there? Is that why they hadn't heard my knocking or my voice? Maybe Dr. Hashigami was in there, busy grading his tests.

Crap. What if he's really here? I hadn't expected that, so my mind was going blank.

But weirdly, the idea of going home had vanished from my mind. I was pretty interested to see what was going on his room. Even if I couldn't get an interview, I wanted to at least get a glance at his seminar room.

Man, I'm such a trend-follower. But that was a good thing, really, if I wanted to run an occult blog.

I knocked on the door in the back, then softly opened it.

There was no one inside it, either. The lights weren't even on.

Once again, all the tension I'd felt was for nothing.

"I knew it. I knew this was going to happen." But if nobody was here, I could take this opportunity to get a look at Dr. Hashigami's seminar room.

This place must be filled with amazing treasures. I probably couldn't write about any of them, though.

If he was this into occult stuff, he must have all kinds of amazing things.

This room was smaller than the seminar room, and it felt like a meeting room or a break room. There was a sofa for guests to sit on. I realized now that this room also had a door connecting to the hallway. Maybe that meant that this was where he talked to visitors.

There was an expensive-looking work desk in the back of the room. On top was a laptop, a mountain of papers, and a lot of what looked like strange objects.

They weren't just any objects, either.

There was a stack of Japanese holy talismans, a hollow paperweight in the shape of a pyramid, a box filled with rune stones, and one of those weird dolls you found in Southeast Asian gift shops. There was even a big crystal ball like you'd see a fortune-teller use in an old anime.

"Yeah, this is what a fortune-teller should be using." I'd never seen a real one before. *Man, I wish I could take a photo. If I could upload this, I'd get a ton of hits.*

It looked like some kind of international occult goods exhibition. There was no organizing pattern at all. But that meant that occult lovers were sure to be interested in it. What caught my eye in particular was what looked like a knife, buried in a stack of papers.

"What is this? Wow! It's so cool!" Even with the only light coming in from the other room, I could tell. The edge of the blade was blue.

I'd seen knives with blue edges on Twitter, come to think of it. It wasn't just a thin layer of blue paint. The blade itself was blue. It was mystical, and really cool looking.

Maybe this was the same type of knife.

Was it some kind of occult thing?

Maybe it was some cursed object from a foreign country.

I couldn't help but pick it up to take a look.

When I held it in my hands, it was heavy. I was surprised at the weight, given its small size. This was no normal knife. Was it a replica made of plaster? Either way, seeing knives was always so cool. Maybe that's just how guys are. It wasn't an occult thing.

I held it with a backhand grip, like a character in a manga.

"Swoosh! Swoosh! Hyper-something-or-other slash!" I swung it around. I wasn't quite sure what the name was supposed to be.

I knew no one was looking, but I was still embarrassed. "What am I doing?" I said to myself, and chuckled. If I didn't chuckle, I was probably going to grab my head and roll on the ground in embarrassment.

Wow, the handle of this knife was really sticky. It was kind of disgusting.

I carefully put it back on the desk, not wanting to touch it anymore. But the sticky sensation clung to my palm.

I looked at my hand in the dim light, and it was stained bright red.

"Huh?" No, it wasn't bright red. It was red and black.

It was sticky, like half-dried paint. It stank a little. *What is this?* I wondered.

I didn't want to think about the answer. My instincts were warning me not to. So I stopped myself from thinking before I came to the obvious answer.

I looked around the room for a tissue, wanting to get this nasty stickiness off my hands as soon as possible.

And then I saw it.

Once I noticed that something was wrong, I couldn't ignore it anymore. I didn't want to look, but I couldn't help it.

I hadn't noticed it when I came inside the room, but, under the desk, on the floor, was a round, bumpy sphere, about the size of a soccer ball.

It looked kind of like a pineapple, but the color was wrong and its shape was rounder. It was so dark that I didn't understand what it was immediately.

The sphere had a human face on it, and there was a neck connected to it, and then a body. Only when I saw that the body was tied to a toppled office chair did I finally understand.

It wasn't a pineapple.

It was a human head, slick with blood, with the scalp ripped off so hard that in some places you could see all the way to the bone.

I remembered the face of Dr. Hashigami, which I'd seen so many times on the TV. He was a man, but he had long black hair that went all the way down to his waist. But more than half of that hair was gone from his head.

Did he rip it off? With his own hands? Or...did someone else do it?

"*Aah... aaaah...*" I almost screamed.

My senses came back to me just in time, and I jammed my upper arm across my mouth.

A tiny little scream slipped out of my mouth. I didn't even realize I was screaming, so it didn't even feel like I was the one screaming.

I felt the strength start to drain from my knees. I felt myself starting to stagger back and fall to the floor.

No. I couldn't fall down here. I needed to stand up and run.

That's what my mind told me. I looked around for something to grab.

What I found was a pile of books on top of the desk. Of course, it wasn't enough to support my weight, so I ended up falling to the floor amid a shower of books.

The warning bells kept going off in my mind.

This was bad. I needed to run. I didn't know why, but I needed to run.

But my legs wouldn't move. It was like my body and mind had split apart. I smacked my useless knees in frustration. And then the paint on my hands—no, it was obvious now that it wasn't paint—stained the pants of my uniform. I had to wash it off. I couldn't let Mom wash it. I had to wash it myself, I thought, and then I found my eyes turning toward the body again.

Was that...Dr. Hashigami? He wasn't moving at all.

Did that mean he was dead? Of course he was dead.

It didn't make sense for him to be tied to a chair. You couldn't do that on your own, which meant that someone else had tied him up.

His face was bumpy and swollen in places, and looked nothing like I remembered it. What could do that to a person? It was barely a human face anymore.

His expression was frozen in pain. I couldn't bear to look at it directly, so I looked away.

But that was a mistake. I saw what was near his outstretched hand.

"No way... This can't be happening..." I froze. There was so much blood right next to his hand.

It was a dying message. Something you often saw in mystery novels. Seeing it in reality, though, just made me sick. A last message from a dead man would be filled with hate and rage. It wasn't something you would want to read.

But it was too late. Now I could never forget it.

The handwriting was shaky, and it was almost hard to be sure that it was really letters.

If you tried to force it to make some sense, this is what it said: "CODE" Which meant— "Hey, you! The stupid-looking guy!"

"!!!!!" I suddenly heard a girl's voice next to me, and literally leapt up in shock.

I leapt up so fast that I ended up hitting my head against the corner of the desk. My body spasmed from the pain.

I was so panicked that I forgot the obvious fact that dead bodies don't talk, and that Dr. Hashigami was a man, and I crawled frantically away from the body.

There was someone besides me and the body in the room! I only came to this terrifying conclusion after I'd already made it to the corner of the room and held my breath, shivering.

But the only place someone could hide in here was behind the

desk. There was a body there, and I didn't see anyone else... I thought.

The door to the other room was closed. Had I closed it? I was the one who opened it. But I didn't remember closing it. I'd been in the room for only two or three minutes now. During that time, I hadn't heard a single sound. I hadn't heard anything from the other room, either. And the voice I'd heard had been really close. It definitely hadn't been coming from the other room.

I wanted to scream, "Who's there?" But it felt like screaming would only make things worse. I was too confused, nervous, and scared to even speak, anyway.

"Why are you panicking?! Get ahold of yourself, dummy!"

"Hyahh!" There it was again. I heard a girl's voice. It was very close.

And it was muffled, like the speaker was wearing a mask.

I looked down at my feet. Of course, there was no one there.

I had no idea where the voice was coming from. My sense of direction and my sense of balance were both gone, and it felt like I'd been thrown into some kind of weird other dimension.

The fear that someone had found me in a room with a dead body started to slowly eat away at me. Then the fear turned into full-blown terror, and the terror stopped me from being able to think.

"Wh-who's there?!" I forced myself to scream.

I looked around the room, again and again and again and again.

"Where... Where are you?!" I should never have come here. I should never have come here to do the interview. I should've stayed in my room like a good NEET. This was all Ryotasu's fault. Why did this have to happen to me?

"What did I do? Waaah!"

"Calm down! Stop crying, dummy!" The girl's voice was

surprisingly close.

Was I really hearing a voice from another dimension?

Was I insane?

Or...

I gulped and took the phone out of my pocket.

Nothing seemed wrong with it. It wasn't even on a call. There was no way it could be coming from here.

Then...the only thing I could think of was my backpack, and the Skysensor I had slung from my shoulder. I gasped.

That's right. That's right!

It was only a few days ago, wasn't it? I'd heard that old song coming from the Skysensor, even though it was turned off?

"No way!" I quickly took the Skysensor off my shoulder and opened the case.

"How long are you going to stay there?!"

"Uwah!"

A bossy girl's voice was coming out of the speaker. It was as if the Zonko strap that was hanging off it was talking. I threw the whole thing away.

The radio landed on the floor, and I could still hear the girl talking. "Don't you understand? If you stay here, they're going to think you're a suspect!"

"What's going on? What station is this? What program is this?"

"This isn't a program! I'm talking to you! You, the one with snot dripping down your nose as you freak out in front of a dead body!"

It was talking to me. The voice from the radio was talking to me. This was impossible. There was no way we could be having a conversation. The Skysensor wasn't a phone. It was a radio.

Wait a minute. Whoever was talking to me knew exactly what I was doing. Why? What kind of magic trick were they using?

"Wh-who are you? Where are you watching me from? Did you kill the professor?!" I grabbed the radio and shouted.

If anybody could see me right now, they'd probably think I looked like an idiot.

I knew that you couldn't do two-way communication with a radio like this, but I was still screaming into the speaker like it was a phone.

"You're about to be caught up in something really dangerous," the girl said to me.

But her words only made me more confused. "Did you set me up?! Why are you doing this? Where are you watching me from?"

"Shut up! Shut up and listen! This is partially your fault for not thinking about what you were doing! You practically asked for this when you came here!"

"Stop yelling and explain—"

"I don't have time! Even if I told you what was really going on, it would take you time to understand it. So I'm skipping it! Got it?!"

"But—"

"Instead, I'm about to tell you something really important. Just do what I tell you."

"Do what—"

"If you want to get out of here safely, then listen to me! Got it?!" The voice on the radio was strong and clearly wasn't going to take no for an answer.

"What should I do?"

"Can you see the toolbox under the desk?"

It was hard to imagine a toolbox being in a room like this. I was sure there wouldn't be one. But still, I looked under the desk, being careful not to glance at the body.

"There it is..." It was a full, professional-grade toolbox. It was weird to see something like that here. "D-did you put that here?" I asked as I pulled the toolbox toward me, but the voice on the radio didn't answer.

"Get out the pliers! Hurry!"

"The pliers? Why do I need pliers? I don't need to bust the lock on the door—"

"Use it to pull out one of the professor's teeth!"

"Wh-what?!"

"Do it!"

I was already enough of a mess. Hearing her tell me that made me start to think I'd be better off passing out and waking up in a holding cell at the police station.

"Wh-what the hell are you talking about? How is pulling a tooth out from a dead body supposed to help me get out of here safely?"

"You want the gold tooth on the far left! Got it? Don't pull out the wrong one!"

"Listen to me—"

"I told you to shut up and listen to me! Do you still not understand the situation you're in? You already touched one of the murder weapons!"

I'd...touched one of the murder weapons? Did she mean the pliers? No, wait!

"That knife!" The knife with the red blade on the desk. Thinking back, it was obvious what that red was now.

That was the murder weapon that killed the professor. And I was stupid enough to grab it and play with it.

"I'm so stupid!" I hated myself. I wanted to punch myself to death, right now.

"Stop wasting time! Somebody will be here soon!" The voice on the radio started to get more tense.

"But... But...I can't pull out his tooth! I *can't!*" I was also curious to know how she knew that someone was coming, but I didn't have the energy left to disobey her anymore.

"Waah... Damn it! Why is this happening?!" I was crying. But I grit my teeth and gripped the pliers hard, then moved toward Dr. Hashigami's body.

"There's a gold tooth on the back left. Just pull it out. There's no time!"

"H-how much time do I have left?"

"About thirty seconds."

"Thirty seconds?!" That was barely any time at all. They were almost here!

"But who—"

"If you've got time to talk, then get started!"

I grabbed the professor's jaw and shivered. It was cold and hard. I didn't realize bodies got so cold and stiff.

I wanted to run away. I didn't want to touch it.

My vision blurred with tears.

"Twenty seconds!" I forced the professor's mouth open. It was harder than I thought, and it took me a little time.

I looked in his mouth. There was a gold tooth shining in the back left.

I forced in the pliers.

I was defiling a corpse.

It felt like the professor's empty eyes were staring at me. I begged him to close his eyes, but it wasn't happening.

My hands were shaking.

It was hard to get the pliers lined up against the right tooth.

"Hurry!"

"I know! Don't hurry me so much!" I finally grabbed the tooth with the pliers.

I pulled, hard. But it didn't budge at all.

"Ten seconds!"

Shit! Shit! Shit! I couldn't do this! This was crazy! I couldn't do something this gruesome! Somebody make it stop! I wanted to cry—

"Five seconds!"

DAMN IT ALL! JUST COME OUT!

I crouched down and stepped on the professor's forehead. With the head pressed firmly against the ground, I pulled on the pliers as hard as I could.

I felt the sensation of ripping flesh in my hands. More blood than I expected came out of the professor's mouth.

I looked down at the end of the pliers, and saw something covered in blood, about five centimeters long.

I wasn't sure what I was looking at.

I didn't realize teeth were so...

"They're here—" Just as the voice spoke, I could hear someone enter the next room.

I shivered and held my breath. Who was it? Who was there? It was obvious it wasn't the girl on the radio.

Then was it the police? One of his students? Or...maybe the

murderer? As best I could tell, there was only one person.

"You can escape if you go now. Go out by the hallway," the radio said.

Whoever they were, the person was still in the seminar room.

I put the bloodstained pliers and the tooth in my bag, not caring about the mess the blood would make. Then I picked up the radio and closed the lid.

And then, my knees trembling, I silently opened the door to the hallway.

The hallway was even darker than when I'd arrived. No one else was here.

I crouched down and headed to the elevators as silently as I could.

I looked back behind me a bunch of times.

What if someone was following me? I was scared. My heart had been pounding hard since I'd found the professor's body. It was so loud I worried the sound would echo down the hall and alert the person in the seminar room.

I made it to the elevators.

There were two elevators. One of them was stopped on the sixth floor. Maybe whoever was in the room now had used it to come here.

I went to press the button for the elevator, and then changed my mind and went for the stairs.

The lights in the stairwell were off, and it was dark. But now, the darkness made me feel better.

I ran down the stairs to the first floor, as fast and as silently as possible.

I made it outside. I was inside the courtyard of Seimei University. No one had followed me.

I wanted to get out of here as soon as possible, so instead of heading for the university's main entrance, I ran toward the high school. I passed two university students on the way, but it was dark now, and they didn't seem to realize that I was covered in blood.

"Hahh... hahh... hahh..." I'd been in the bathroom for about twenty minutes, washing the blood off. I'd deliberately kept the lights off.

"It's a curse... All the bad deeds I've ever done... I've been punished for them."

Maybe it was because the black magic agency had cursed me, I thought to myself. I should never have sent Ryotasu there.

But hiding in Seimei High was the right move. Most of the clubs were done for the day, and the only room with a light on was the teachers' office.

I'd run into the furthest bathroom on the third floor of the special classrooms building, where no one was likely to go, and started to wash off my hands.

"I can't...get the stink off..." The blood was gone, but it felt like I could still smell a metallic stench.

I kept rubbing with soap, again and again and again.

There were spots of blood on my uniform. I couldn't get it totally clean here, but I should at least clean it with water. I'd have to wash it carefully once I got home, or my mom would find out. I had to be careful.

There was a stain on the knees of my pants that was too big for me to come up with an excuse. If I got anywhere near Kichijoji station like this, the cops were sure to stop me.

I had no choice but to strip down to my underwear and wash my pants in the sink.

It was just a school sink, so there wasn't any hot water. I kept washing them with cold water until my fingers went numb. I could barely feel my fingertips anymore. But I kept washing.

All kinds of questions filled my mind, but I refused to think about them. If I did, my brain would burst.

What happened? What did I just get caught up in? Who killed the professor, and why? Who had come into the room after me?

And more than anything...who was the voice that I'd heard from the radio?

The Skysensor had been dead silent since I'd left the university. I'd been too busy washing my hands and clothes to look, but I'm sure if I did I'd find that the power switch was off, just like it was when I'd heard "Gloomy Sunday."

Was that voice real? If it was, maybe I was hearing things. That would make me like a psychic.

I'd managed to make it out of there because of the voice, after all. But there were a lot of things the voice said that didn't make sense.

"Oh, right... What do I do with this gold tooth?"

I'd been so desperate to get out of there that I'd thrown the pliers and the tooth in my bag. The bag was lying on the ground at my feet. It was covered in blood, too.

"I have to wash it off. I have to wash off all the blood..." I rummaged through my bag.

The blood on the pliers and the tooth had stained some of my textbooks.

That alone was enough to make me regret doing it, and I felt sick thinking about the fact that I had even more cleanup to do.

I took the tooth and the pliers out my bag.

"Grrr..." The tooth was still stuck to the pliers. I removed it. Just touching it made me feel sick.

This was obvious, but it had been inside Dr. Hashigami's mouth. Just the thought of touching it disgusted me.

I couldn't carry it around when it was covered in blood, though. I forced myself to bring it over to the sink and wash off the blood.

I rubbed the blood off with my fingers. There were little chunks of flesh stuck to it in parts, and it made me want to throw up.

I felt guilty for doing this. This was desecration of a corpse. I was desecrating Dr. Hashigami's very dignity as a human being.

"What's going on? What the hell is going on?" I kept washing the tooth, trying not to throw up.

The root of the tooth had little depressions in it, and those depressions in particular were filled with little pieces of flesh. I bit my lip and carefully cleaned each one.

The dark red blood and chunks of flesh went down the drain. Little by little, the surface of the tooth became visible.

And eventually, I saw it. When I did, I turned on the lights, not caring who saw me.

It was so bright that for a moment, I couldn't see. My vision came back quickly, and I looked down at the tooth.

"No way. Is this..."

Gold teeth were normally just put over the top of your real tooth. My mom had some teeth made of silver, so I knew that.

But this tooth was different. It wasn't a real tooth. It was an implant.

So the root of the tooth that had been inside the professor's gums was also made of metal.

It had a weird shape. Just looking at it was enough for me to tell what it was. I couldn't believe what I was seeing.

"This... This is a key, isn't it?"

There was a tiny key, about 5 centimeters long, buried in the professor's mouth.

I felt cold sweat run down my back, and I shivered inside the cold bathroom.

≫ KIRIKIRI BASARA

Official Name: "Paranormal Science Kirikiri Basara." An occult aggregator blog run by Yuta Gamon. Every day, he picks occult-related news stories for his readers to disprove scientifically.

≫ EGGS

Throwaway accounts made on Twitter for the sole purpose of attacking and slandering others. Their owners never reveal who they are, and when things turn bad, they'll quickly abandon the account and flee. For this reason, it's extremely common for them to not set a picture for their icon, which means they use the default picture—an egg.

≫ CAFÉ☆BLUE MOON

A café and bar tucked away five minutes from Kichijoji Station. During the day, it's a café, and at night, it's a bar. The place is decorated in an extremely Oriental fashion that suits its owner's tastes, and it can be difficult for first-timers to enter. Yuta brings his laptop here to update Kirikiri Basara.

≫ WOODBERRYS

A frozen yogurt shop that opened in Kichijoji in 1997. It offers homemade yogurt and farm-fresh fruits. In addition to frozen yogurt, there's also yogurt drinks, yogurt scones, and yogurt soap available as well.

≫ SUTA-DON

A pork bowl that's the most popular item at the rice bowl chain called "The Legendary Suta-Don Store." Suta-Don bowls are known for being far larger than the bowls offered by competing chains. Suta-Don is, therefore, short for "stamina bowl."

≫ SIMULACRA PHENOMENON

The phenomenon where any three points in an upside-down triangle shape will tend to be seen as a human face. Patterns in animal fur, wood knots on ceilings, and shadows cast by rocks in satellite imagery are all common examples of this.

≫ KOKKURI-SAN

A form of fortune-telling that uses, or appears to use, a supernatural phenomenon very similar to the Western ouija board. Many people believe that it is a form of spiritual summoning that involves summoning the spirit of a fox. In kanji, it's written Ko (Fox), Ku (Dog), Ri (Raccoon). It's always done with two or more people. A paper with the words "yes," "no," "torii" (an arch at the entrance to a shinto shrine), "man," "woman," the numbers one through nine, and every letter of the Japanese alphabet is put on a desk. Then a ten yen coin is placed on the paper, and all participants put their index fingers on the coin. After an incantation, a question is asked of Kokkuri-san, and the coin is said to move on its own to answer the question.

» ONE-MAN HIDE AND SEEK

An urban legend that became popular in the 2000s. It's considered another form of spiritual summoning, like Kokkuri-san. The ritual is done in the dead of night, and involves repeatedly playing hide-and-seek (or rather, performing a ritual that seems similar to it) with a stuffed animal whose stuffing has been removed and replaced with white rice and your own fingernails. This ritual is repeated again and again for an hour or two. It's said that there was a rumor that strange paranormal events would happen during this ritual, and many people started to do it for fun.

» NICO LIVESTREAMER

A regular user of the Niconico Livestreaming service. Some livestreamers can be extremely popular.

» SKYSENSOR

A portable radio sold to the general population in the 1970s. In addition to AM and FM, it can also receive shortwave broadcasts. It has a lot of other functionality as well, and was a big hit.

» QSL CARD

Also known as a verification card. A card issued by a TV or radio station as proof that you received a broadcast. Listeners can receive a broadcast and submit a report to the station, which will reply with this card. Each station has its own card design, so some dedicated collectors exist. However, since there's no legal requirement to send a QSL card, some stations don't.

≫ NICONICO LIVESTREAMING

A livestreaming service offered by the Niconico video site. In addition to official programs run by the site staff, there are also livestreams broadcast by regular users. Since anyone can easily upload a user livestream, there are many of them held every day, and their contents range from simple small talk to coverage of very niche hobbies.

≫ SPR

The Society for Psychical Research. Founded in 1882 at Trinity College in London. An academic society founded to promote scientific research into spiritualism and the paranormal. It researches six subjects of study: telepathy, hypnosis, poltergeists and other spiritual manifestations, ghosts, spirit-summoning, and the history of the paranormal. At the end of the 20th century, advances in science greatly accelerated scientific research into the paranormal, and the SPR, which had been in decline for some time, returned to the public eye.

≫ AHRIMAN

One of the dolls Aria uses in her rituals. It has a green striped body and bug eyes. Its name comes from the god who rules over evil itself in the Zoroastran religion.

≫ GORGON

One of the dolls Aria uses in her rituals. It has a yellow and black pattern like a honeybee, and the face of a dog. Its name comes from the three ugly sisters of Greek mythology, Stheno, Euryale, and

Medusa.

≫ COVEN

One of the dolls Aria uses in her rituals. It has five eyeballs and its body is covered with stars. Its name comes from a word used to describe a group of witches since the latter half of the sixteenth century.

≫ PETER

One of the dolls Aria uses in her rituals. It has a bright purple body and multicolored fabric teeth. Its name comes from one of the twelve apostles of Jesus Christ, who later became a saint.

≫ LILITH XII

One of the dolls Aria uses in her rituals. Its head is covered with a paper bag. A prince of black cats who lost its tail. Its name comes from a woman in the Book of Genesis who was Adam's first wife, and who later became the wife of the fallen angel Lucifer.

≫ AMENITY DREAM

A chain of trading card stores with fourteen locations around the country. They often hold tournaments in their stores.

≫ VANGUARD

Full name: *Card Fight Vanguard*. A trading card game made by Bushiroad. "Lead knights, dragons, mecha and angels, dinosaurs and mermaids! Stand at the Vanguard and fight in this one-on-one card game!" (From the official site.)

≫ ICPO

International Criminal Police Organization. Also called Interpol.
An international organization which counts police from 190
countries among its members. The organization's primary function
is to facilitate cooperation between police in different countries by
helping them exchange information and issue international warrants.
It has no police officers of its own, and most of its staff are office
workers.

≫ SUPER ULTRA LUCKY TEA

An original drink created by the owner of Café ☆ Blue Moon. It was
so awful that Yuta was in serious pain after drinking it, but the owner
himself says he likes it.

≫ *KYAM-KYAM*

A fashion magazine for women in their 20s. It primarily deals with
work, femininity, and girly fashions, and its articles on tips for
dressing for work and attracting men are loved by readers.

≫ DON'T MISS IT POM!

A news and information variety program broadcast Monday through
Friday.

≫ HOT READING

A technique used by self-proclaimed fortune-tellers and psychics
when they perform "readings" of a target. "Hot reading" is the
act of gaining information on a target in advance. By giving out
information that only the target and those close to him should know

during the reading, the fake psychic can gain the target's trust.

≫ RAMEN SABURO

A ramen shop in front of Seimei University. It was originally named something else, but someone drew graffiti on their sign, and that's how it got its present name.

≫ *MUMUU*

A monthly occult magazine. Founded in 1979, it has over thirty years of history.

≫ 666

The number of the beast, found in the Revelation of John in the New Testament. The number has also come to be associated with devils and devil worship.

≫ *MASTER MUST MURDER*

Yuta's favorite late-night anime. Its abbreviation is MMM. A suspense and crime action show with lots of pretty girls' blood flying everywhere. Yuta particularly likes the heroine, Zonko.

≫ THE TREE OF LIFE

A symbolic diagram used in Kabbahlic mysticism. It consists of ten spheres with twenty-two channels between them and is said to represent the universe and the human body.

PARANORMAL SCIENCE NVL
Occultic;Nine
オカルティック・ナイン

THERE IS NO SUCH THING AS THE "OCCULT." IT CAN ALL BE DISPROVED BY SCIENCE.
ONLY THOSE WHO HAVE ACCEPTED EVERYTHING
HAVE THE RIGHT TO KNOW THE TRUTH.

Afterword

Readers of Overlap Novels, members of that group of maniac fans of Chiyomaru Shikura, as well as the Committee of 300—thank you for reading. This was my first time writing a light novel, and it was difficult in many ways, but we've managed to successfully release it.

I'd like to take this opportunity to thank all of the staff who worked on this project with me.

Now, how did you enjoy the first volume? It would make me happier than anything if there was something inside that got stuck in your mind in even the smallest way. To be honest, though, I'm not satisfied with it at all! I mean, who wants a novel that ends like this? Man, I hated to end it this way. I could've gone on for 1,500 pages if they'd let me.

My stories are always incredibly long to begin with. All the descriptions are rambling, and a lot of it isn't needed at all.

I realized when I was working on this that pro authors are a whole different breed, aren't they? They write exactly what they need to and no more. Their stories are beautiful and polished, like a poem, and the scenes go naturally from one to another. My stories aren't like that at all. I'm no good. No good at all, no.

Just typing in all this text is making me feel depressed. What should I do? I should talk about something else.

I know. I'll talk about something that readers would probably enjoy. Some kind of behind-the-scenes thing...

Like I just said, the stories I write are really rambling. Most of the big reveals tend to take place in the second half, and I don't reveal much about who's really behind things. I always think that if some big villain shows up all of a sudden, it makes things feel fake and less real.

I thought about this problem up until the last minute for this book, and right before the deadline, I added in the scenes marked "MMG."

In other words, they didn't exist not that long ago, lol. I'm not sure if adding them was the right thing to do, but this work has a lot of information in it, and my goal this time was to keep that information from being tilted too much in any one direction. If I reveal too much, they'll probably get mad at me, but the ideology motivating the villain this time is vast in scale, and something big enough that it could potentially deny all the world's religions.

Of course, since I've called this a "science" novel, it can't just be cheap fiction. It takes place in a very plausible timeline, so I hope you'll look forward to the latter half. If any reader can guess their ambitions from what's been revealed so far, send me a message on Twitter.

I'll ask you to delete it immediately, lol.

Now, since I'm here, I may as well talk about some things other than the villain. The scariest part of the book is the prologue, isn't it?

You know, the scene where piles of bodies are being pulled from the lake in Inokashira Park. What was that? It's hard to be sure if it was a dream, or real.

But if you look at the world news, you'll see scary phrases like "mass hysteria" and "mass suicide." Most of these are the result of mind control, or religious groups with twisted ideologies. Will that be the case here?

Since this is the most critical part of the book, of course I can't talk about it in the afterword. So look forward to the last half of the story! Lastly, a word about the special powers the protagonists have. The devil in Aria's part especially seemed to speak in an everyday, slangy manner, didn't it?

Was that really a creature that could be explained by science? Or was it some sort of pinpoint fantasy? Keep that in mind, as well.

Oh, of course, it's also equally likely that this afterword itself is an attempt to mislead the reader, too.

Also, was there anything else in Volume 1 that stuck out at you as a potential plot point or foreshadowing?

If there was, tell me on Twitter. I'll ask you to delete it, too.

Anyway, that's all the time we have! I'm praying for the end of summer (I hate summer) as I get to work on the second and further volumes of *Occultic;Nine*.

See you next time! Poh-yah-yah me on Twitter!

—Chiyomaru Shikura

PARANORMAL SCIENCE NVL

Occultic;Nine
オカルティック・ナイン

THERE IS NO SUCH THING AS THE "OCCULT." IT CAN ALL BE DISPROVED BY SCIENCE.
ONLY THOSE WHO HAVE ACCEPTED EVERYTHING
HAVE THE RIGHT TO KNOW THE TRUTH.

Volume 2: COMING SOON